How to write an

IMPRESSIVE
CV

&

COVER LETTER

Visit our How To website at **www.howto.co.uk**

At **www.howto.co.uk** you can engage in conversation with our authors – all of whom have 'been there and done that' in their specialist fields. You can get access to special offers and additional content but most importantly you will be able to engage with, and become a part of, a wide and growing community of people just like yourself.

At **www.howto.co.uk** you'll be able to talk and share tips with people who have similar interests and are facing similar challenges in their lives. People who, just like you, have the desire to change their lives for the better – be it through moving to a new country, starting a new business, growing their own vegetables, or writing a novel.

At **www.howto.co.uk** you'll find the support and encouragement you need to help make your aspirations a reality.

You can go direct to **www.how-to-write-an-impressive-cv-and-cover-letter.co.uk** which is part of the main How To site.

How To Books strives to present authentic, inspiring, practical information in their books. Now, when you buy a title from **How To Books**, you get even more than just words on a page.

How to write an

IMPRESSIVE
CV

&

COVER LETTER

A comprehensive guide for the UK job seeker

TRACEY WHITMORE

howtobooks

Published by How To Books Ltd,
Spring Hill House, Spring Hill Road,
Begbroke, Oxford OX5 1RX, United Kingdom
Tel: (01865) 375794, Fax: (01865) 379162
info@howtobooks.co.uk
www.howtobooks.co.uk

How To Books greatly reduce the carbon footprint of their books by
sourcing their typesetting and printing in the UK.

First published 2009
Reprinted 2010
Reprinted 2011

British Library Cataloguing in Publication Data
A catalogue record for this book is available from the British Library

ISBN 978 1 84528 365 0

Produced for How To Books by Deer Park Productions, Tavistock
Typeset by Kestrel Data, Exeter, Devon
Printed and bound by Bell & Bain Ltd, Glasgow

NOTE: The material contained in this book is set out in good faith for
general guidance and no liability can be accepted for loss or expense
incurred as a result of relying in particular circumstances on statements
made in the book. Laws and regulations are complex and liable to change,
and readers should check the current position with the relevant authorities
before making personal arrangements.

CONTENTS

INTRODUCTION

This book is dedicated primarily to help you write your own effective, interview-winning CV and cover letter, and begins by providing an insight into the whole job-acquisition process.

JOB-HUNTING PROCESS

When searching for a job, there is a distinct process that needs to be followed. It begins with mentally preparing yourself for change and ultimately ends in a job offer. Each of the steps involved in the process are discussed at length, and include useful job-hunting tactics. The section concludes with some very useful job-hunting tips.

CV WRITING

Your CV is your 'marketing tool' and the way you present yourself to a prospective employer can be the difference between you getting an interview and your CV being binned. Having a targeted, well-polished, professional CV to differentiate you from the crowd has never been so important.

You only get one chance to make a first impression, to open doors and win interviews, so you have to get it right first time. After determining the CV type that will best suit your skills and experience, this book takes you through a step-by-step process on how to produce your masterpiece. It covers everything from how to head your CV in the most effective way through to how to present the information to achieve maximum impact. It is all about making facts easy to find, highlighting them to your best advantage and being careful not to undersell or oversell yourself.

COVER LETTERS

Cover letters are often overlooked; if done correctly, they can set you apart from the competition. Hence, the importance of using your cover letter as an extension of your CV is covered in depth. This section details how to construct both speculative and tailor-made cover letters to 'turn on' your specific audience, and how to add a personal touch to a very factual document.

TRIED AND TESTED EXAMPLES

CV and cover letter writing is an art form and too many people get it wrong, but art can be copied! As such, real life examples of successful CVs and cover letters have been used throughout this book. Many of these job seekers were struggling to secure interviews and needed serious help. It can be useful to examine their existing 'failing' and revised 'winning' CVs.

EXPERT OPINIONS

As part of my research, I met with senior human resources professionals from blue-chip organisations to glean an insight into the whole job acquisition process and what they look for in a candidate's CV. Interviews were conducted with leaders at Goldman Sachs, Vodafone, KPMG, Tesco, BBC and Mars Drinks; the Managing Director and Managing Partner of two of the UK's largest executive search firms Korn Ferry and Odgers, Ray and Berndtson; and a talent scout and head of practice at Jonathan Wren, part of the Adecco Group which is the largest staffing company in the world.

CD

The appended CD includes many, many examples of CVs and cover letters across all levels and industries, and numerous CV and cover letter templates that you can use to produce your own impressive documents. The templates are easy to manipulate and to personalise. Additionally, full transcripts with all 12 industry experts are included as an appendix on the CD.

My aim was to produce a book that would appeal to the widest audience and one that would be easy to follow. I am confident that this has been achieved.

Wishing you all the best in your job search.

ABOUT THE AUTHOR

Originally from South Africa and degree educated, I have spent the last nine years in the UK, seven of which have been in recruitment. In 2001, I worked as an executive search consultant for a leading Surrey-based executive search firm and spent two years recruiting a variety of candidates into key blue-chip organisations within the financial services, pharmaceutical and insurance sectors.

In 2003, I felt ready to set up and run my own business. Applying valuable knowledge gained from the recruitment industry and through conducting extensive research, Impressive CVs was launched. I have been writing CVs across the board since 2003 and employ several freelance CV writers, all of whom come from a recruitment or HR background. Impressive CVs has an excellent track record of producing interview-winning CVs and cover letters for customers at all levels, across all industries and has an undisputed list of excellent testimonials.

What gives me my buzz is helping people achieve their dreams and aspirations; I have managed to accomplish this over and over again in the last seven years and I am proud to have made a difference to so many peoples' lives.

ACKNOWLEDGEMENTS

Writing this book has been a year long process, but well worth it and I take this opportunity to thank my freelancers Linda Baldwin, Sue Bryant, Kay LaRocca, Jo Lamb, Yvette Segal and Katie Slater, and my customers who have all kindly granted me permission to publish their documents as examples throughout my book and on the appended CD, to which you will surely benefit. Those who wished to be personally acknowledged include Nicholas Forder; his CV and cover letter can be found on the appended CD. Where real life CVs or cover letters have been used, all personal details of the individuals concerned and any companies they have been affiliated with, have been removed to protect their identities.

As part of the process, time was spent interviewing HR professionals from a variety of blue-chip organisations, executive search firms and an agency, to make sure no stone was left unturned. I thus take this opportunity to thank those HR professionals who afforded me their time. They have provided me with an invaluable insight into the job market and what they look for in a CV; I am certain you will find their input extremely useful.

A big thank you goes to Nikki Read at How To Books for agreeing to publish my book, and in such a short space of time.

Last, but most importantly, I would like to thank my husband, Charlie for his continued support; my angel, Cade, who is always a source of inspiration; Bump; my parents, Lyn and Laurence, and brother Paul, who have always believed in me; my friends and family.

It has always been my ambition to leave something behind when I am gone and now, this is a dream that has been realised.

HOW TO USE THIS BOOK

Begin by reading Part One and getting to grips with the job-hunting process.

Once you have identified your target position and bridged any skills gaps, you can proceed to Part Two, which takes you through the process of creating your own CV. To achieve the best results, it is recommended that you have a pad of paper to hand so that you can make notes at each step. These notes, in conjunction with CV examples and CV templates provided on the CD, are what you will use to compile your CV. When writing your CV, refer to the 385 action words at the end of the book for inspiration.

Once you have identified an opportunity, proceed to Part Three. Read through the entire chapter before putting pen to paper. Once you have determined whether you require a speculative or a specific letter, refer to the specific sections that relate to your requirements. Select a template from the appended CD and refer to examples on the same for inspiration.

By the time you have finished reading this book and reviewing what the CD has to offer, you should have the framework for a truly great CV and cover letter, and a good understanding of how to approach the job-hunting process.

Before sending out your CV and letter, ensure they are both targeted to the role in question.

Note: Examples, quotes and comments made by industry experts are all expressed in boxes.

HOW TO USE THE INTERACTIVE CD

The interactive CD attached to this book includes material to help you produce your own impressive CV and cover letter: **CV and cover letter examples** that have worked in real-life that will provide you with inspiration, and **CV and cover letter templates** that can be used to create your own CV. The CD also contains full transcripts of interviews that the author has held with twelve industry experts, providing valuable advice and insights.

1. **To view the cover letters and CV examples** you will need **Adobe Acrobat Reader** or **Professional**, version 5 or above. If you don't have Acrobat Reader installed on your computer, you can download the latest version free from http://get.adobe.com/reader. Installation usually takes less than five minutes.

2. **To use the cover letter and CV templates** you will need **Microsoft Word®**, version 1997 or above.

To access the material on the CD:

1. Place the disk in your CD drive and, when it appears on your desktop, open the file entitled **1. IMPRESSIVE CD START.PDF** by double clicking. Ignore the folder All Documents, as this contains the resources accessed through the PDF.

2. The interface window, **Interactive CD Guide**, opens in Acrobat Reader and a navigation panel on the left will allow you to access the Word templates and the PDF samples (in red). Double clicking on a link will open either a PDF in a new window, or a Word® template. You can ignore any warnings about potentially harmful programs, macros, or viruses. The Word® templates are editable to enable you to create your own CV and cover letter but the PDFs are not.

Part One

The Job-Hunting Process

CHAPTER I

HOW TO APPROACH JOB HUNTING

Job hunting is defined as the act of looking for employment due to unemployment or discontent with a current position. The goal of job hunting is to obtain an interview with an employer and, ultimately, an offer of employment. Job acquisition, if done properly is a full-time job. There is a distinct process that needs to be followed, which is detailed below:

Mentally Prepare
↓
Determine Target Position
↓
Bridge Skills/Qualification Gaps
↓
Prepare CV
↓
Identify Jobs/Make Contacts
↓
Prepare Cover Letter
↓
Interview Stage
↓
Job Offer
↓
Embrace Change

This chapter examines each of these steps. Preparing your CV and cover letters are covered in detail in the next two parts of the book.

STEP 1: MENTALLY PREPARE

The first step to job hunting is mentally preparing yourself for two things:

1. **To open a new chapter in your life.**

   Changing job needs to be viewed as a positive, life-changing experience, and you need to focus on how your life will benefit from this change. You will face new challenges, meet new people, learn new things and new ways of doing things. Be prepared to adapt and embrace the possibility of change.

2. **For the realities of the job-hunting process.**

   Finding a job is a job in itself. Devote time, energy and passion to the process and do not be tempted to cut corners. If you are unemployed, treat it as your new job. If you are employed, treat it as your second job.

   Job hunting is stressful and it is easy to become despondent. Keep sight of your goal and your employment value, but be flexible and be prepared to pursue alternative options. Along the way, you may discover other more appealing roles. In a competitive environment you may, out of necessity, need to accept a job that does not meet all of your career preferences, and you may need to treat it as a stepping-stone to something better.

STEP 2: DETERMINE TARGET POSITION

The most difficult part of finding a job is often deciding what that job should be. Without a goal in mind it can be difficult if not impossible to realise your dream.

If you don't know where you are going, how can you expect to get there?
Basil S. Walsh

Without goals and plans to reach them, you are like a ship that has set sail with no destination.

Fitzhugh Dodson

Before you begin your search, define your employment values and be clear about the kind of position that you are looking to secure.

Answer the following questions about yourself:

- What motivates you?
- What are you passionate about?
- What are your priorities?
- What skills, knowledge and experience do you posses?
- What do you like most/least about your current job?
- What do you want more of; what do you want less of?
- What do you want to change?
- What factors in life are most important to you?

> ❝ The first thing is to really think through what is it you want to do and why. It is really important to think about what you enjoy and what you're good at and really be clear in your own head about what type of career you're looking for. Mapping out some sort of a life vision of where you want to go is really important. ❞
>
> *Mark Thomas at Tesco*

> ❝ Find out what really motivates you and what motivates you is often what you enjoy doing. If you can discover that, your life will be much richer as a result, in all areas. ❞
>
> *Giles Crewdson at Korn Ferry*

This can be achieved in the following ways:

Self-assessment – Examine each question based on what you know about yourself.

Peer/management assessment – Ask people who know you well, on both a professional and personal level, to provide feedback on each area. Also revisit old performance appraisals as these can be very informative.

Self-help methods – Utilise career guidance books or employ the services of a career coach. Consulting with a professional can be very enlightening as they have experience of assessing career options and determining realistic career goals and strategies. They can also help to build or rebuild confidence.

External assessment – Complete standardised tests and exercises that are designed to help you make better career choices. Psychometric testing can be undertaken online, through colleges, universities, or through private career counselling services. Another option is to access online job sites: input your core skills into their search criteria and assess the results of possible job matches.

After giving these questions some serious thought, determine your job-hunting objectives:

1. Prepare a list of job titles that best describe your talent and which utilise the skills and experience that you have;
2. If you are looking for something completely different, identify whether there are any skills or qualification gaps;
3. Identify the industry and type of employer you would like to work for.

STEP 3: BRIDGE SKILLS OR QUALIFICATION GAPS

Should you not have all the skills, qualifications or experience required to undertake a particular role, it may be necessary to upskill. Upskilling may also be necessary to improve your employment prospects. This can be achieved in two ways:

1. **Training** – It may be necessary to complete a particular qualification, in which case you would need to enrol on a course.
2. **Gaining experience** – Consider voluntary work; not only would you gain the necessary experience and some valuable contacts, but also a useful insight into whether the career you have earmarked is really the right one for you.

STEP 4: PREPARE YOUR CV

This step is covered in detail in Part Two. It covers the importance of having a targeted, well-polished, professional CV and provides step-by-step guidance on how to prepare an interview-winning CV.

STEP 5: FIND A JOB

Once you have prepared your CV, the next step is to begin identifying opportunities and applying for roles. As mentioned earlier, job seeking is a full-time exercise and, as such, you need to be proactive, organised and tenacious.

Below are six ways to identify potential opportunities:

1. Networking

Effective networking is central to any active job search. There are three areas to concentrate on:

(a) Contacts

Pursue both people you know and people you don't know. There is your professional network of current and former colleagues, and then your private network made up of friends, family and those people you have met socially at non-work functions. Determine who would be most influential and maintain regular contact with them.

> *I would definitely tap into my personal network before sending out my CV left, right and centre to recruitment agents and I'd probably keep it quite targeted.*
>
> Louise Mayo at KPMG

(b) Networking sites

Join business and social networking sites such as:

- www.linkedin.com
- www.XING.com
- www.facebook.com
- www.viadeo.com

- www.spoke.com
- www.plaxo.com
- www.ryze.com

Many organisations, including headhunting firms and agencies, trawl these regularly to identify new talent.

> **Tip**
>
> **Potential employers may 'google' candidate names as part of due diligence and reference checking; inappropriate photos/comments on sites like Facebook can be very damaging.**

(c) Attend events

Regularly attend careers fairs, seminars and conferences where you are likely to meet new or existing contacts.

Be relentless in your networking activities because the famous saying in business still holds true today, *'it's not what you know it is who you know'*.

2. Targeting specific companies

Making a direct approach to a company, whether through a contact or speculatively, can be an excellent way of finding out about opportunities that are not yet in the public domain.

(a) Named contact

If you have been provided with a lead, write to your contact in the first instance, sending them your CV and cover letter. Follow up in a week to 10 days with a phone call to determine how best to progress your application.

(b) Speculative approach

If you are approaching companies speculatively to see what opportunities may exist for someone with your skills and experience, identify a targeted list of companies that you would like to work for and research each one. Establish who the correct contact would be; in smaller companies aim for the hiring authority or Human Resources Director; in larger organisations, contact the

Head of Resourcing or Head of Talent to determine the correct contact. Once you have a name, email your CV and cover letter to the appropriate contact. Follow up with a phone call a week or two later.

Many companies are very open to receiving applications on spec and as such, this is a very good way of getting your details in front of them.

3. The internet

The internet is a powerful tool to jump-start your job hunt. Not only does it provide you with access to employers' career sites, but it is a research tool that provides you with access to an infinite amount of information on companies, industries, professions and much more.

(a) Targeting specific companies

If you have a specific company in mind, visit their website. Most UK companies use online recruitment as part of their strategy to attract potential candidates. This is a relatively easy way to determine what opportunities are available and may even highlight possibilities you had not previously considered. If there is nothing immediately suitable, some company websites allow you to opt for job alerts via email. As mentioned in point two above, you could always send your CV on a speculative basis.

(b) Job boards/job sites

Job boards are a mainstream part of the recruitment process for job hunters seeking work and for employers or recruiters seeking qualified candidates.

Job seekers have the option to search for jobs online. Most job boards allow you to search by keywords, occupation, salary level, preferred geographic location, and job type (permanent, part-time, temporary or contract). When inputting your key skills, some interesting alternatives may present themselves.

With some job sites and job boards, once registered, you can opt for job alerts via email. You also have the option of uploading your CV. This makes it easy for you to apply for jobs, and for employers or recruiters to access your information and contact you if your details are of interest to them.

The most popular job boards are:

- www.monster.co.uk
- www.jobsite.co.uk
- www.cv-library.co.uk
- www.fish4jobs.co.uk
- www.totaljobs.co.uk
- www.jobserve.co.uk
- www.reed.co.uk

It is often worth identifying specialist or niche job boards that are specific to your occupation or industry.

4. Recruitment agencies

Many agencies have a reputation for treating you as a number and for providing little or no value to your job search. Albeit, recruitment consultants are a valuable source of information as it is their job to be informed about what is happening in the job market. They have contacts with major companies across a range of industries, they have direct access to many jobs and if you find the right agent, they can save you a lot of time and effort.

The key is to find the right agent to represent you. Speak with friends and colleagues as perhaps they can refer you to a consultant. It is more valuable to receive a referral to a specific consultant than to a specific agency. Seek out niche agencies that specialise in your industry or sector, as specialist agencies are likely to understand your skills and experience, and will be in a better position to guide you. As a result, they are more likely to put you forward for roles that are a good fit. Focus on forging a strong relationship with your consultant, as the kind of relationship you have with them will determine your success and how quickly you will find the job you are looking for.

When registering with agencies, register with no more than two or three. If a consultant knows you are registered with many agencies, they are likely to allocate less time to you and your job search. Another reason is that agencies may send your CV to clients unsolicited. If you have many agencies representing you, it is possible and quite likely that your CV could end up on someone's desk more than once. This makes you look desperate and over-exposed in the market.

'*Candidates only need one or two good consultancies that can represent them to the companies they want to work for. There is no benefit going out to five to ten different agencies, having one's CV registered with different people – candidates will lose track of where their CV has gone and it can become very embarrassing.*'

Sean O'Donoghue at Jonathan Wren

5. Head-hunters/executive search firms

For candidates earning in excess of £60,000 it is well worth approaching a select number of executive search firms to ascertain whether any of their clients are looking for someone with your skills and experience. Head-hunters operate at the top end of the market and are often retained by blue-chip organisations to tap into the market and secure top talent. Most head-hunting firms are open to receiving CVs on a speculative basis but you need to be aware that unless they have an opening for you at this moment in time, you are likely to be placed on to their database and will only be contacted should something suitable come up in the future. Search firms are focused primarily on fulfilling their clients' needs and, as such, they will not spend time searching out a role for you. Consequently, it is worth contacting several head-hunters who specialise in your industry or sector.

6. Newspapers and trade publications

Although online postings are a more common form of advertising, many companies still continue to place advertisements in the local/national press and in trade publications, so this can be another good source of jobs.

Looking through the recruitment sections of these publications can often provide you with some interesting possibilities.

Tip

In order to reduce the amount of time spent searching for a job, you need to have a 'few irons in the fire'. Do not be tempted to use one method and apply for just one role. Be proactive and apply for two to three jobs each week. In the same token, do not 'carpet bomb' the market for reasons mentioned earlier.

STEP 6: PREPARE YOUR COVER LETTER

Part Three covers this topic in detail, from the importance of including a cover letter with your application, through to how to prepare an interview-winning letter for a specific role and on spec.

STEP 7: INTERVIEW STAGE

If you have a well-written, targeted CV and cover letter, and you are a good match for the role, you are likely to be short-listed and contacted for interview.

Should you not hear from the agency or company within 10 days of applying for a job, contact the employer or recruitment professional to enquire about the status of your application. If you are not invited to interview or if you are rejected at interview stage, obtain feedback as you can build on this.

STEP 8: JOB OFFER

At this stage, you either accept or reject the offer. Just because you are offered the role does not mean you have to accept it. Give it some serious thought and speak with family members and friends before making your final decision.

Should you opt to accept the position, contact the person who offered you the role to thank them and inquire about the proper protocol involved in starting your new job.

STEP 9: EMBRACE CHANGE

If you have elected to accept the offer, you will be feeling one of two things: excitement or fear; perhaps a combination of both. Both these emotions are good and totally normal.

I'm not afraid of storms, for I'm learning to sail my ship.

Louisa May Alcott

Change is the law of life. If we look at this in the context of the recruitment industry, individuals who change jobs every few years are likely to develop and progress their careers more quickly than those who stay put. People who become comfortable and complacent cannot grow as they are not stretching themselves or their boundaries. People often resist change because they are scared of failure and they do not want to become less useful than they aleady are. Unless you keep abreast of change, your skills can lose their edge and even become obsolete. Often change involves adapting your style, your thought pattern and being willing to learn and accept new ways of doing things.

> *I think new challenges are good and if you can go into different organisations, take away their best practices and then come into another organisation and share those best practises, I think it's great.*
>   Bindu Sudra at KPMG (Management Consultancy)

For companies, it is important to constantly have fresh talent joining them as this brings new ideas and innovative ways of thinking to their organisation.

> *There's a lot more movement than there used to be. It's seen to be a very healthy thing.*
>   Will Dawkins at Odgers, Ray and Berndtson (Executive Search Firm)

Change is scary but it is the secret to success. Look at change as an opportunity to learn and grow.

Continue to the next chapter for some important job-hunting tips.

CHAPTER 2

JOB-HUNTING TIPS

Below are some important tips that will help you through the whole job acquisition process:

1. **Job acquisition is a full-time job**; treat it as such and you will be rewarded.

2. **Keep your search targeted**
   Rather than applying for 50 roles, find five that meet your requirements 100% and that match your skill set 100%. Spend time adapting your CV and cover letter to each role that you apply for. This will increase your odds significantly.

3. **Be flexible**
   In a competitive environment, it may be necessary to compromise on some aspects of the roles that you apply for.

4. **Be organised and record everything you do**
   Keep a log of all your applications including dates, contact details, and the outcome.

> ❛ *It needs to be a planned activity and what's really important is keeping records of what you've sent to whom, so when people start contacting you have a record of everything.* ❜
>
> *Anna Tomkins at Vodafone*

5. **Attend all interviews**
   Attending interviews, unless the role is a really bad fit, builds confidence and it is a good learning experience. Become 'interview fit'.

6. **Prepare hard for each interview**

   Find out what the structure of each interview is likely to be and prepare accordingly. Research the company and the role prior to interview. Show enthusiasm for the company and the role throughout the process.

7. **Get feedback**

   If you are unsuccessful at CV or interview stage, find out why as this can be very valuable for future applications and you can build on this.

   Contact the employer or recruitment professional one to two weeks after sending off your application or, if there is a closing date, one to two weeks after the closing date. Follow up interviews within two days.

8. **Stay motivated**

   Whether you are not being invited to as many interviews as you had anticipated or whether you are being rejected at interview stage, you have to realise that job-hunting is both time-consuming and emotionally draining. It is very natural and easy to lapse into a negative spiral and be tempted just to give up. Stay focused and be patient.

❛ *You also need to have realistic expectations; it can take time regardless of the role, your level or what you're looking for.* ❜

Anna Tomkins at Vodafone

Keep positive, remain focused on the goal and believe that you will be successful. The good things in life are never easy.

❛ *The difference between a successful person and others is not a lack of strength, not a lack of knowledge, but rather in a lack of will.* ❜

Vincent T. Lombardi

Happy job hunting!

CHAPTER 3

STAYING MARKETABLE

Once you have started in your new job, it is important to actively manage your own career. The job for life culture is a thing of the past; nowadays, it is not up to a company to develop you, it is up to you to invest in your own career. This is increasingly important in a competitive environment.

Job security comes from within and is your ability to find a job rapidly should the need arise. You need to invest time and effort into staying marketable, allowing you to respond quickly to a tight market or to a new opportunity.

To progress and stay ahead of the competition, you need to:

1. **Stay abreast of changes in your industry and market** – Read relevant industry magazines, and attend seminars and conferences regularly;
2. **Keep your network alive** – Consistently build and maintain your professional network; this is crucial to your ongoing marketability. It keeps you abreast of new opportunities and of changes in or outside your area of expertise;
3. **Professional development/upskill** – Complete industry specific qualifications and courses, whether external or internal.

It is easy to become stuck in a rut – it is comfortable, but don't do it!

Part Two

CV Writing

CHAPTER 4

YOU HAD BETTER GET IT RIGHT!

To appeal to prospective employers, you need a targeted, well-polished, professional CV that differentiates you from the crowd. A CV is your 'marketing tool' and the way you present yourself to a prospective employer can be the difference between you getting an interview and your CV being binned. The next 18 chapters will take you through a step-by-step process of putting together an interview-winning CV. Before we begin, let's discuss exactly what a CV is, why it is so important to get it right, what the experts have to say and the importance of keeping it truthful.

WHAT IS A CV?

A Curriculum Vitae is Latin for *'the course of one's life'* and is defined by the Collins Dictionary as *'an outline of a person's educational and professional history, usually prepared for job applications'.*

THE IMPORTANCE OF GETTING IT RIGHT

When looking for a job, regardless of profession, you will usually be asked for your CV. A CV is used to help a prospective employer determine your fit for the role and is your first communication with the prospective employer. As you are often competing against hundreds of applicants, your CV needs to stand out in terms of both layout and content. To compromise on the quality of your CV will only compromise your chances of securing an interview.

Recruitment professionals are often the first point of entry. If you are responding to an advertisement, it is very likely that they will be making the decision on which candidates will make the shortlist. Should you be applying speculatively, it will again be their decision as to whether to put you forward to a hiring authority or to one of their clients. Consequently, they are the people you need to impress.

Most people postpone writing their CV until the very last minute and do not afford their CV the time and attention it deserves. It is somewhat apparent from reading the comments below that too many people underestimate the importance of a CV and do a rushed and an inadequate job.

WHAT THE EXPERTS SAY ABOUT THE CURRENT STATE OF CVS

'CVs are hit and miss. We end up having to modify seven out of ten CVs we receive.'

Jonathan Wren (Recruitment Agency – Sean O'Donoghue)

'CVs are 'poor to average''

KPMG (Management Consultancy – Sean Jowell)

'Very bad.'

Tesco (Retailer – Mark Thomas)

'Typically the CVs received are generally quite good, but with a pretty high degree of variation.'

Goldman Sachs (Investment Bank – Jonathan Jones)

'Typically CVs are unfocused, not commercial and not scannable. On the whole, people are stuck in a different era when it comes to CVs.'

BBC (Broadcaster – Daniell Morrisey)

STRETCHING THE TRUTH

CVs need to be factual. Do not be tempted to stretch the truth or tell half-truths. Minor embellishments or lying can be the worst mistake you can make on your CV.

'*If you say you had an MA when it was a BA, or you went to Business School without pointing out the fact that you didn't graduate, that looks to the client as if you're lying. It's not really a lie, it's sort of a half-truth isn't it; but the impact on your reputation is terrible. If you get caught doing it once, it sticks.*'

Will Dawkins at Odgers, Ray and Berndtson

'*Most large companies these days undertake various forms of background checking between the point when somebody is offered a job and when they actually start. Part of this will indeed include validating that what you have represented on your CV is correct – so it's very important to make sure that it's all watertight and above board.*'

Jonathan Jones at Goldman Sachs

CONCLUSION

In a market that is becoming more and more competitive, it has never been more important to have a first-class but factual CV. A step-by-step process of how to achieve this is covered in the subsequent chapters. With each step you take, you are one step closer to securing your dream job.

CHAPTER 5

DETERMINING THE MOST SUITABLE CV TYPE

In order to grab the reader's attention and increase your chances of being invited to interview, you need to have a CV that best represents your skills and experience. As such, it is vital that you select the CV type that will portray your skills and experience in the best possible light.

The three CV types are identified, defined and discussed, and an example of each is provided.

CHRONOLOGICAL CV

Defined
The definition of *chronology* as defined by the Collins dictionary is '*the determination of the proper sequence of events*'.

As the definition suggests, a chronological CV provides a detailed account of your career history and educational history in order. The information needs to be presented in reverse chronological order, i.e. most recent information first.

When to use a chronological CV
- You have a solid career history in a particular field, industry or discipline.
- You have no major time gaps between positions.
- You have worked for well-known companies with good reputations and have held impressive job titles.
- You are looking to highlight your most recent jobs.
- You have clearly defined career goals.

Advantages of a chronological CV
- A chronological CV is considered to be the traditional approach and is the most commonly used CV type.

Example of a chronological CV

Melissa Stewart

123 Silver Street, Leighton Buzzard, Bedfordshire LU7
Tel (h): +44 1234 567 890
Email: melstewart@abcd.co.uk

PROFESSIONAL PROFILE

A highly professional, confident and ambitious individual, with over eight years' commercial experience within a variety of roles including airline cabin crew, PR and document management. Self-motivated, reliable and diplomatic, with a proven ability to multi-task, working calmly and rationally under pressure while maintaining a positive attitude. Good humoured, approachable and friendly, seeking to provide a high quality of customer service at all times, working discreetly and meticulously. Displays high levels of integrity, a strong team player who also enjoys a degree of autonomy and independence.

KEY SKILLS

- **Communication** – Possesses excellent interpersonal, presentation and public speaking skills; highly perceptive and quickly able to develop relationships with customers and colleagues
- **Customer Service** – Proven ability to interpret individual requirements, defuse difficult situations, and create a positive environment for customers
- **Problem Solving** – Applies initiative and creativity to resolve difficult situations, utilising limited facilities available to compensate for any technical or personal problems experienced by customers
- **Organisation** – Adept with planning, prioritising and scheduling tasks efficiently, and handling multiple demands. Able to quickly evaluate situations and adapt to changing situations
- **Relationship Management** – Engenders trust by displaying absolute integrity in all transactions
- **Language** – Conversational French; currently learning Arabic with basic skills in sign language
- **IT** – Proficient user of MS Word, Excel and PowerPoint using a PC or Mac

ACHIEVEMENTS

- Represented the company at various prestigious events, including press and media meetings for new product launches and rugby sporting events in Edinburgh during Spring 2007 (CAT)
- Played an active role in effectively managing an emergency landing situation, utilising fire-fighting skills during an incident over the Atlantic en-route to New York (TGA)
- Escorted British Civil Aviation Authorities on selected aircraft test routes as an ambassador for TGA Airlines, when purchasing new aircraft (TGA)
- Achieved all monthly targets for onboard Duty Free sales, receiving regular awards and management recognition (TGA)
- Secured over 700 new customer contract signings during a single 12-hour shift, against a target of 300, for their Phones4U client (BRR Associates)
- Streamlined the organisation of the microfilm division, through re-evaluating an eight-month backlog within a period of just two months (ABC Bank)

CAREER HISTORY

Aug'03–Present   **CAT Airline, Hayes**
Senior Flight Attendant

- Provide a high quality of service to First Class Business travellers, ensuring their safety, entertainment and catering requirements are all managed efficiently

- Supply silver service to customers and assist the cockpit crew
- React quickly and calmly to defuse and prevent escalation of potential customer complaints or difficult behaviour
- Active role model in the training of junior cabin crew in safety and security procedures
- Supervise a team of between four and eight junior cabin crew in Economy class, with a passenger load of up to 300 customers

Sept'00–Aug'03   **GA Airlines Airways, London**
                               Senior Flight Supervisor

- Joined TGA as a Junior member of the Cabin Crew, progressing to a senior role after two years, supervising a team of four junior members of the cabin crew
- Attended to many high-profile clients in a discreet and confidential manner

Sept'00–Aug'03   **BRR Associates, Bournemouth**
                               PR Representative

- A part-time position, representing blue-chip companies at PR events
- Provided information to the general public and applied skills of persuasion to achieve promotional sales targets

Sept'99– Sept'00   **ABC Bank plc, Surrey**
                               Microfilm Supervisor

- Interviewed, selected and trained a team of five staff to manage and organise the daily flow of documents into the office using an improved design system
- Headed monthly corporate presentations and conferences on business productivity and profit to an audience of senior/regional managers from all UK offices
- Controlled all relevant and significant documents entering the department daily

Pre-1999
Early career as a Hair Stylist and Colour Technician in the UK

EDUCATION AND TRAINING
CBC & Group Classes in Management, CAT College, Hayes, 2007–2008
Modules included: Motivating teams, Assertiveness, Business Writing, Problem Solving, Providing Feedback, Coaching, Managing Difficult People, Superior Customer Service, Leading the Way and Resolving Conflict.

Ecology Diploma, The British School of Yoga, 2007
World Religion Diploma, The British School of Yoga, 2007
IATA Airline Marketing Diploma, CAT College, Hayes, 2006
City & Guilds NVQ 1,2 & 3 Hair & Beauty, Kingston College, Surrey, 1994–1997
9 GCSEs including English and Mathematics

VOLUNTARY WORK
- 24-hour member of the Worldwide Emergency Assistance Team, specialising in critical aviation emergencies
- Provided administration skills for an ABC charity, which achieved its registration as an official charity in the UK in October 2005
- Teacher's Assistant at ACA Special Needs school during 2004
- Volunteered at RCA Rehabilitation Centre in the UK for children recovering from major accidents from 2000 to 2003
- Completed a sponsored skydive to raise funds for the National Asthma Campaign and Multiple Sclerosis organisations in 2001

References: Available upon request

- It is the preferred choice of most recruitment professionals and the most widely recognised.
- It is a good way of showing progression and growth.
- It complements a continuous career history within the same discipline.

FUNCTIONAL CV

Defined
The definition of *function* as defined by the Collins dictionary is '*the intended purpose of a person or thing in a specific role*'.

As this definition suggests, when producing a functional CV, identify what your strengths and skills are in relation to the role you are applying for. Therefore, this CV type focuses on your transferable skills in relation to your target position.

When to use a functional CV
- You are changing career or work direction into a different field, industry or discipline.
- You are applying for a job where you have little or no previous relevant experience.
- You have a chequered work history.
- You have been in one job or industry for a very long time.
- You do not have direct experience to the role to which you are applying.
- You have significant gaps in your career.
- You have held several very similar positions.
- Your career has downsized or you are looking to take a step back.
- You want to emphasise work or achievements from your early career.
- You have been recently absent from the job market.
- You have had several very different jobs.
- You have frequently changed employer.
- You are concerned about your age – dates can customarily be eliminated from this CV type.

Advantages of a functional CV
- It accentuates your transferable skills.
- It enables you detract attention away from your career history.

Example of a functional CV

Melissa Stewart

123 Silver Street, Leighton Buzzard, Bedfordshire LU7
Tel (h): +44 1234 567 890
Email: melstewart@abcd.co.uk

OBJECTIVE

Seeking to utilise the skills gained across a variety of environments to secure a role as a Team Leader in a customer-focused environment.

PROFESSIONAL PROFILE

A highly professional, confident and ambitious individual, with over eight years' commercial experience within a variety of roles including airline cabin crew, PR and document management. Self-motivated, reliable and diplomatic, with a proven ability to multi-task, working calmly and rationally under pressure while maintaining a positive attitude. Good humoured, approachable and friendly, seeking to provide a high quality of customer service at all times, working discreetly and meticulously. Displays high levels of integrity, a strong team player who also enjoys a degree of autonomy and independence.

KEY SKILLS

Communication
- Possesses excellent interpersonal skills, highly perceptive and quickly able to develop relationships with customers and colleagues
- A good listener, with well developed presentation and public speaking skills

Customer Service
- Skilled with interpreting individual requirements and providing an empathetic approach at all times
- Experienced with providing a high quality of service to First Class Business travellers; ensured their safety, entertainment and catering requirements were all managed efficiently
- Accustomed to reacting quickly and calmly to defuse and prevent escalation of potential customer complaints or difficult behaviour
- Attended to the needs of many high profile clients in a discreet and confidential manner

Leadership and Training
- Proven ability to create and maintain a positive and motivational environment for both customers and staff alike
- Experienced with supervising teams of between four and eight cabin crew, with a passenger load of up to 300 customers
- Selected as an active role model in the training of junior cabin crew in safety and security procedures
- Headed monthly corporate presentations and conferences on business productivity and profit to an audience of senior/regional managers from all UK offices
- Interviewed, selected and trained a team of five staff to manage and organise the daily flow of documents into the office using an improved design system

Problem Solving
- Applies initiative and creativity to resolve difficult situations, utilising limited facilities available to compensate for any technical or personal problems experienced by customers

Organisation
- Plans, prioritises and schedules tasks efficiently, maintaining objectivity in difficult situations and handling multiple demands and competing priorities

- Able to navigate through a multitude of issues, to recognise and evaluate situations, define a clear way forward, actively adapting to changing situations

Relationship Management
- Engenders trust by displaying absolute integrity in all transactions
- Demonstrates a concern for harmony and a friendly environment

ACHIEVEMENTS

- Represented the company at various prestigious events, including press and media meetings for new product launches and rugby sporting events in Edinburgh during Spring 2007 (CAT)
- Played an active role in effectively managing an emergency landing situation, utilising fire-fighting skills during an incident over the Atlantic en-route to New York (TGA)
- Escorted British Civil Aviation Authorities on selected aircraft test routes as an ambassador for TGA Airlines, when purchasing new aircraft (TGA)
- Achieved all monthly targets for onboard Duty Free sales, receiving regular awards and management recognition (TGA)
- Secured over 700 new customer contract signings during a single 12-hour shift, against a target of 300, for their Phones4U client (BRR Associates)
- Streamlined the organisation of the microfilm division, through re-evaluating an eight-month backlog within a period of just two months (ABC Bank)
- Joined TGA as a Junior member of the Cabin Crew, progressing to a senior role after two years, supervising a team of four junior members of the cabin crew

CAREER HISTORY

Aug'03–Date	**CAT Airline, Hayes** **Senior Flight Attendant**
Sept'00–Aug'03	**TGA Airlines Airways, London** **Senior Flight Supervisor**
Sept'00–Aug'03	**BRR Associates, Bournemouth** **PR Representative**
Sept'99–Sept'00	**ABC Bank plc, Surrey** **Microfilm Supervisor**
Pre-1999	**Hair Stylist and Colour Technician**

EDUCATION AND TRAINING

2008 **CBC & Group Classes in Management, CAT College, Hayes**

Modules included: Motivating teams, Assertiveness, Business Writing, Problem Solving, Providing Feedback, Coaching, Managing Difficult People, Superior Customer Service, Leading the Way and Resolving Conflict

2007 **Ecology Diploma**, The British School of Yoga

2007 **World Religion Diploma**, The British School of Yoga

2006 **IATA Airline Marketing Diploma**, CAT College, Hayes

1997 **City & Guilds NVQ 1, 2 & 3 Hair & Beauty**, Kingston College, Surrey

1995 **9 GCSEs** including English and Mathematics

IT SKILLS
Proficient user of MS Word, Excel and PowerPoint using a PC or Mac

LANGUAGES
Conversational French; currently learning Arabic with basic skills in sign language

CHRONO-FUNCTIONAL CV

A chrono-functional or combined CV mixes the elements of a chronological and a skills-based CV, borrowing the best features from each of the other two styles. The chronological CV provides a detailed account of your career history and educational history whilst the functional CV provides a detailed account of your transferable or core skills. Hence, the combined CV provides a combination of skills, career and educational history, but in less detail.

When to use a chrono-functional CV

- You want to emphasise both skills and career history.
- You have a solid career history in a particular field, industry or discipline.
- You have no major time gaps between positions.
- You have worked for well-known companies with good reputations and have held impressive job titles.
- You are looking to highlight your most recent jobs.
- You have clearly defined career goals.
- You have been in one job or industry for a very long time.
- You are applying for a job where you have little or no previous relevant experience but have an impressive career that you do not want to hide.
- You do not have direct experience to the role to which you are applying, but as above, you have an impressive career that you do not want to conceal.
- You have held several very similar positions.

Advantages of a chrono-functional CV

- You are able to highlight both your transferable skills and your career history.
- You are still able to show progression and growth.
- Some believe this is the most effective CV format.

Example of a chrono-functional CV

Melissa Stewart

123 Silver Street, Leighton Buzzard, Bedfordshire LU7

Tel (h): +44 234 567 890

Email: melstewart@abcd.co.uk

PROFESSIONAL PROFILE

A highly professional, confident and ambitious individual, with over eight years' commercial experience within a variety of roles including airline cabin crew, PR and document management.

Self-motivated, reliable and diplomatic, with a proven ability to multi-task, working calmly and rationally under pressure while maintaining a positive attitude. Good humoured, approachable and friendly, seeking to provide a high quality of customer service at all times, working discreetly and meticulously.

Displays high levels of integrity, a strong team player who also enjoys a degree of autonomy and independence.

KEY SKILLS

Communication
- Possesses excellent interpersonal skills, highly perceptive and quickly able to develop relationships with customers and colleagues
- A good listener, with well developed presentation and public speaking skills

Customer Service
- Exceeds all expectations in an assured, impressive and unhesitating manner through interpretation of individual requirements, provision of personal assurance and an empathetic approach at all times
- Creates and maintains a positive and motivational environment, providing a great atmosphere and service for all customers

Problem Solving
- Applies initiative and creativity to resolve difficult situations, utilising limited facilities available to compensate for any technical or personal problems experienced by customers

Organisation
- Plans, prioritises and schedules tasks efficiently, maintaining objectivity in difficult situations and handling multiple demands and competing priorities
- Able to navigate through a multitude of issues, to recognise and evaluate situations, define a clear way forward, actively adapting to changing situations

Relationship Management
- Engenders trust by displaying absolute integrity in all transactions
- Demonstrates a concern for harmony and a friendly environment

Language
- Conversational French; currently learning Arabic with basic skills in sign language

IT
- Proficient user of MS Word, Excel and PowerPoint using a PC or Mac

ACHIEVEMENTS

- Represented the company at various prestigious events, including press and media meetings for new product launches and rugby sporting events in Edinburgh during Spring 2007 (CAT)
- Took an active role in effectively managing an emergency landing situation, utilising fire-fighting skills during an incident over the Atlantic en-route to New York (TGA)
- Escorted British Civil Aviation Authorities on selected aircraft test routes as an ambassador for TGA Airlines, when purchasing new aircraft (TGA)
- Achieved all monthly targets for onboard Duty Free sales, receiving regular awards and management recognition (TGA)

- Secured over 700 new customer contract signings during a single 12-hour shift, against a target of 300, for their Phones4U client (BRR Associates)
- Streamlined the organisation of the microfilm division, through re-evaluating an eight-month backlog within a period of just two months (ABC Bank)

CAREER HISTORY

Aug'03–Present   **CAT Airline, Hayes**
Senior Flight Attendant

- Provide a high quality of service to First Class Business travellers, ensuring their safety, entertainment and catering requirements are all managed efficiently
- Provide silver service to customers and provide assistance to the cockpit crew
- React quickly and calmly to defuse and prevent escalation of potential customer complaints or difficult behaviour
- Active role model in the training of junior cabin crew in safety and security procedures
- Supervise a team of between four and eight junior cabin crew in the Economy class, with a passenger load of up to 300 customers

Sept'00–Aug'03   **TGA Airlines Airways, London**
Senior Flight Supervisor

- Joined TGA as a Junior member of the Cabin Crew, progressing to a senior role after two years, supervising a team of four junior members of the cabin crew
- Attended to many high-profile clients in a discreet and confidential manner

Sept'00–Aug'03   **BRR Associates, Bournemouth**
PR Representative

- A part-time position, representing blue-chip companies at PR events
- Provided information to the general public and applied skills of persuasion to achieve promotional sales targets

Sept'99–Sept'00   **ABC Bank plc, Surrey**
Microfilm Supervisor

- Interviewed, selected and trained a team of five staff to manage and organise the daily flow of documents into the office using an improved design system
- Headed monthly corporate presentations and conferences on business productivity and profit to an audience of senior/regional managers from all UK offices
- Controlled all relevant and significant documents entering the department daily

Pre-1999
Early career as a Hair Stylist and Colour Technician in the UK

EDUCATION AND TRAINING

CBC & Group Classes in Management, CAT College, Hayes, 2007–2008
Modules included: Motivating teams, Assertiveness, Business Writing, Problem Solving, Providing Feedback, Coaching, Managing Difficult People, Superior Customer Service, Leading the Way and Resolving Conflict

Ecology Diploma, The British School of Yoga, 2007
World Religion Diploma, The British School of Yoga, 2007
IATA Airline Marketing Diploma, CAT College, Hayes, 2006
City & Guilds NVQ 1,2 & 3 Hair & Beauty, Kingston College, Surrey, UK, 1994–1997
9 GCSEs including English and Mathematics

VOLUNTARY WORK

- 24-hour member of the Worldwide Emergency Assistance Team, specialising in critical aviation emergencies
- Provided administration skills for an ABC charity, which achieved its registration as an official charity in the UK in October 2005
- Teacher's Assistant at ACA Special Needs school during 2004
- Volunteered at RCA Rehabilitation Centre in the UK for children recovering from major accidents from 2000 to 2003
- Completed a sponsored skydive to raise funds for the National Asthma Campaign and Multiple Sclerosis organisations in 2001

References: Available upon request

THE CV TYPES COMPARED

Chronological and the combined CV are the CV types that most people are familiar with and as per our panel of experts, are the preferred format. The functional CV is considered to be the 'black sheep' of the CV family – it is not conventional and it raises concerns that you have something to hide. Most of those interviewed added that they found functional CVs both difficult to read and hard to follow.

> ‘ If it comes in a chronological order, to me that's a complete jigsaw that you've built and I can see it. ’
>
> *Anna Tomkins at Vodafone (Telecommunications)*

> ‘ *I do think they have their place. From a personal preference point of view, my key principle is that past performance predicts future performance, so the essence of a CV for me is again about key achievements rather than necessarily skills that led to those achievements.* ’
>
> *Mark Thomas at Tesco (Retailer)*

Warning

If you had decided that a functional CV was your best option, you may now be tempted, after reading the above, to keep to the more conventional CV types. Do not discount the functional CV as it can be very useful in a variety of situations and it may very well be the best CV type for your situation. Choosing the wrong CV type will dramatically reduce your chances of being selected for interview.

> ‘ *A skills-led CV is entirely appropriate for some roles – healthcare professionals, project managers or professional interims, for example.* ’
>
> *Anna Tomkins at Vodafone*

> ‘ *If a candidate is confident they can do the job but they do not have the exact work experience the employer is looking for, they can consider a functional CV.* ’
>
> *Sean O'Donoghue at Jonathan Wren*

Tip

For those with less than two years' experience, you should consider a chronological or a chrono-functional CV type. If you have no previous work experience, part-time or other, consider a one-page CV.

Once you have selected your CV type, proceed to the next chapter. If you are still unsure about which type would be most suitable, why not review some of the examples on the appended CD.

CHAPTER 6

HEADING YOUR CV

Your CV needs to be headed with your name and contact information, and as such, heading your CV is step one of the CV writing process. Each area is now discussed in detail and is followed by what to exclude.

1. **Your name**
   - ■ It is necessary to include your first and last name only.
   - ■ If you have a unisex or unusual name, include your title, such as Ms, Mr, Miss.
   - ■ It is acceptable to include letters after your name if your qualification is relevant to the role being applied for.
   - ■ Ensure that you name is the focal point, so centre it and use a large font size – point 18 or 20.

2. **Address**
   Beneath your name, include your full address. Do not be tempted to use abbreviations, i.e. Herts instead of Hertfordshire or Rd instead of Road.

3. **Contact details**
   Next, include all your contact details, i.e. home and mobile telephone numbers and your personal email address, as this makes it easy for a prospective employer to contact you. Ensure the contact details you provide are up-to-date and that your email address is suitable.

> *Things like an appropriate email address are important because when people don't provide contact details, it is very frustrating.*
>
> *Leila Bliss at KPMG*

EXAMPLES OF HOW YOUR CV SHOULD BE HEADED

Example 1:

Tracey Whitmore BCom

14 Westwood Drive, Harpenden, Hertfordshire AL5 4KT
Tel: (h) 0123 456 789 (m) 07123 456 789
Email: traceywhitmore@abcd.co.uk

Example 2:

JAMES WEST

5 Silver Street, Eastleigh   Tel: (m) 07123 456 789
Hampshire SO52   Email: jwest@abcd.com

WHAT HEADINGS TO EXCLUDE

People are often enticed into adding titles, logos, work contacts and photographs. The reason why each of these should not be included is discussed below.

1. **Titles**
   Do not be tempted to include a title on your CV such as: 'Curriculum Vitae', 'CV' or 'Resume' as by the time you are finished producing your CV, it will be obvious what the document is.

2. **Logos**
   Some people feel the need to include logos of courses they have completed or company logos. Do not do it. One, it takes up valuable space and two, when documents are scanned, faxed or emailed, logos can cause problems because they are not readable or, in the worst case scenario, information can be lost.

3. **Work contact details**
   Avoid including your work telephone number or email address unless you have very good reason to do so. It is unprofessional as you do not want prospective employers or agencies contacting you at work; it may result in your employer getting wind of the fact that you are looking to move.

4. **Photographs**

The trend today is against photographs; they take up a lot of space and they say nothing about your ability to do the job.

Some of the experts interviewed believed that including a photograph was one of the biggest mistakes you could make on your CV:

Unless you've specifically been asked to provide a photograph in your CV, steer away from it. Particularly in the UK, I don't think employers really want to see a photo, in particular, a funny photo.

Anna Tomkins at Vodafone

In my opinion, no matter how hard you try, you make a judgement based on the photograph someone includes on their CV.

Sean Jowell at KPMG

Tip

Be sure to head the second and each subsequent page of your CV with your name and most appropriate contact number. Should your CV be received or distributed as a hardcopy, it is possible that the pages can become separated.

CHAPTER 7

CAREER OBJECTIVE

Step two of the process is to detail your career objective. A career objective is a personal statement that defines what you are looking to achieve in your professional life, and its purpose is to express to a potential employer what it is that you are looking to do.

A Technologies Graduate looking to secure a challenging support position within a forward thinking, progressive ICT-technology orientated company.

Experienced specialty carpenter seeking to exploit extensive trade skills gained in the construction and special events industries, in order to secure a management position.

WHEN TO INCLUDE A CAREER OBJECTIVE
Including a career objective is not mandatory and only needs to be included in the following circumstances:

- your experience is diverse;
- the role you are applying for is very different to your last/current role;
- you are looking to draw on experience from your early career;
- you are a graduate or entry-level job seeker;
- you are producing a functional CV.

If you have a solid career history and are applying for a job in the same line of work or are looking to make the next obvious step up, then it is not necessary to include one and you can proceed to Chapter 8.

EXPERT OPINION
Some experts interviewed felt career objectives are best discussed at interview:

> ‘ My personal view is I'd prefer to explore that with the person either over the phone in terms of a first conversation or at interview, and as we go through the process understanding more about them, their aspirations and their direction. ’
>
> Anna Tomkins at Vodafone

> ‘ Career statements, I'm not so sure about to be honest. I think that's probably more for discussion at interview rather than necessarily on a CV. ’
>
> Mark Thomas at Tesco

A recent survey, however, indicated that 40% of employers like to see an objective, which is quite a convincing reason for using one, so if in doubt, include one.

THE BENEFITS OF A CAREER OBJECTIVE

A career objective is important for the following reasons:

- it can help to clarify your career goals;
- it helps provide focus to a CV;
- it shows a prospective employer that you have direction;
- it allows you to tailor your CV to a specific job;
- it serves to quickly inform your employer what you have to offer.

You often get just 30 seconds to grab the reader's attention so if it is not clear from the outset why you are suitable for the role in question, there is the distinct possibility that your CV will be binned.

WHAT SHOULD A CAREER OBJECTIVE INCLUDE?

Career objectives need to be specific but not limiting and should include:

- what qualifications, skills and/or experience you have to offer;
- what position you are pursuing;
- what your career goal or aspirations are.

TIPS ON WRITING A CAREER OBJECTIVE

- Express what is in it for the potential employer, i.e. 10 years' sales experience.
- Endeavour to include a 'job title' wherever possible.
- If you are applying for a specific role, mirror one/two words used in the advertisement and tailor your objective to the role being applied for.
- If you are making a speculative approach, keep your objective specific but not constrictive and let the employer know what you have to offer.
- Keep it concise; no more than two sentences.
- Tell the employer what you can contribute, i.e. demonstrate your value to the organisation.
- Avoid using 'I'.
- Be truthful.

EXAMPLES – LESS THAN TWO YEARS' WORK EXPERIENCE

As a first time job seeker, you have very little experience to draw upon and your studies or work experience may have very little to do with your target position or career aspirations. As such, it is necessary to make it very clear from the onset what your target position and/or aspirations are and what you feel you could contribute to a prospective employer. As such, most graduate or entry-level CVs should include an objective.

Following the completion of a BSA Degree, seeking to pursue a career in Event Management working for a progressive organisation that rewards commitment, dedication and hard work.

Seeking to utilise relevant work experience to secure a position as a Development Specialist or Finance Analyst working for a leading Real Estate organisation.

Recent high school graduate with previous experience gained in the retail and leisure industries, aiming to pursue a full-time position as a sales representative.

To secure an internship with a leading law firm in order to gain practical experience and further develop existing skills and knowledge.

Seeking to secure part-time employment making use of varied experience gained in the entertainment and leisure sectors whilst continuing to study towards a Media Studies diploma.

To utilise and develop skills and knowledge gained from a mathematics degree, to secure a challenging and progressive entry-level position with a leading investment bank.

To work with highly technical software or hardware applications in a customer centric environment.

EXAMPLES – MORE THAN TWO YEARS' WORK EXPERIENCE

The reason someone with your level of experience will be looking to include a career objective will be because your next step will not be obvious. Hence, provide a summary of what you have to offer and your target position.

Seeking to secure a challenging position as a <Job Title> in order to complement and develop existing competencies, skills, education and experience in Business and Finance.

Eager to pursue a career within IT System Support, building on newly acquired skills attained from MCSA and through various technical support positions.

An accelerated learner and self-starter pursuing an opportunity as a <Job Title>, within a dynamic, forward-thinking organisation offering opportunities to progress intellectually, personally and professionally.

Looking for a Financial Analyst position within fund management, in a role that will best utilise strong mathematical and analytical skills.

With over 20 years' experience in website development and data information systems, now seeking to secure a similar international management appointment.

Seeking to draw upon the skills and experience gained across a variety of roles to secure a role in Customer Services.

A self-motivated, dedicated and driven individual seeking to secure a Trainee Position with a reputable firm of Solicitors following the successful completion of the Legal Practice Course.

With over 10 years' commercial experience gained in customer service, training, sales and administration positions, seeking to secure a position that will further develop client-facing experience.

Looking to secure a role as a Maintenance Technician or Mechanical Engineer drawing upon technical expertise and knowledge gained in the RAF.

Following the recent completion of a Certificate in Quantitative Finance, now seeking to utilise the skills and experience gained in Engineering and through studies to transition into Derivative Sales.

To excel within an IT Technical Support position, building on skills and knowledge attained following the completion of a Bachelor's degree in Computing and previous work experience.

To utilise strong interpersonal and people skills, coupled with commercial experience gained in both the financial services and utilities sectors, to secure a position within Training and Development.

WRITING YOUR CAREER OBJECTIVE

Now that you are armed with what to include and have several examples to draw upon, select a heading from the ones below and begin working on your own career objective. For more inspiration, refer to the appended CD.

Titles: This section can be entitled 'Career Objective', 'Objective' or 'Career Statement'.

> **Tip**
>
> If you choose to include an objective, the balance of your CV should focus on supporting this objective and convincing a prospective employer that you are capable of achieving it.

CHAPTER 8

PROFILE STATEMENT

Step 3 of the process is to create your profile statement. A profile statement is used to paint a picture of who you are and as such needs to provide a short summary of your background/experience, skills and achievements. It provides you with an invaluable opportunity to 'sell' yourself. Just as the purpose of an advertisement is to get people to buy, a profile statement is your opportunity to hook the reader's interest.

*An ambitious **Graduate** with a **First-Class Bachelor's Degree in Tourism & Hotel Management** and two years' commercial experience gained in the hotel and leisure industries. Commended for being highly organised, driven and productive with a resolute approach to entrusted tasks. Reputed as energetic and motivated; thrives on working in fast-paced environments and as part of a team.*

*A highly professional **Service Delivery Manager** with six years' progressive experience working in the oil and gas industry. As an enthusiastic, assertive and motivated individual with strong multi-tasking and problem-solving skills, has successfully aided the implementation and running of a new in-house software system. Possesses key leadership qualities, including lateral thinking, empathy and reliability and thrives on undertaking new and exciting challenges.*

Your profile statement should appear directly below your objective; if no objective has been included, then directly after your name and contact information.

EXPERT OPINION

A recent survey undertaken by CMC (Career Management Consultants Limited) showed that 90% of HR specialists believe that a short profile or summary is useful on the first page of a CV. Our industry experts had this to say:

> ❝ I think a profile statement at the top of a CV as a brief summary which sums up the essence of that person can be quite helpful as it can be compelling to the reader. It can create greater interest, it can make you stand out and differentiate you from others. ❞
>
> *Tesco (Retailer) – Mark Thomas*

> ❝ One sentence is fine; there is no need to list a string of qualities as it means very little. These type of qualities will shine through at interview. ❞
>
> *KMPG (Management Consultancy) – Bindu Sudra*

> ❝ Everyone will tend to describe themselves as a smart, driven and capable person, and therefore it seldom is a point of differentiation; arguably you run more risk of doing yourself harm with something like that. ❞
>
> *Goldman Sachs (Investment Bank) – Jonathan Jones*

Whether to include a profile statement and how much information to include, is an area of contention but it is my recommendation to include one. Like everything else with your CV, it needs to be done well. Your profile statement must be a differentiator and it needs to be convincing.

CONTENT

Your profile statement is likely to be the first thing that a prospective employer will read, so it is imperative that it creates an impact and holds the reader's attention. It should highlight your unique selling points and should be kept punchy, concise, relevant and interesting.

The questions you need to ask yourself are:

1. **What are your core attributes?** Dedicated, results-driven and enthusiastic.
2. **Who are you?** A financial analyst.
3. **What is your experience, past and present?** Ten years' investment banking experience.
4. **What are your core skills?** Highly numerate with superb planning and organisational capabilities.

5. **What areas do you specialise in or what are your areas of expertise?**
Working with small corporates with turnover of up to £10m per annum.
6. **What have you achieved or in which areas do you excel?** Developing
client accounts and increasing revenue.
7. **What do you enjoy doing?** Team leading, client contact.

*A dedicated, numerate and highly sought-after **Financial Analyst**
with 10+ years' experience gained working for two of the UK's leading
investment banks. Experienced with managing and developing a portfolio
of small corporate accounts with annual turnover of circa £10m,
and positively impacting bottom-line profitability. Thrives on providing
exemplary levels of customer service and managing small teams.
Enthusiastic and results-driven with an innate ability to pay close attention
to detail.*

TIPS ON WRITING A PROFILE

1. **Keep it credible** – There is nothing that irks a reader more than big,
powerful words and statements that cannot be validated in your CV. Avoid
using attributes that cannot be substantiated, for example, declaring you
are a leader but are unable to provide demonstrable examples. Another
example is to use words like ambitious and hardworking, but providing no
evidence of the fact.
2. **Keep it factual** – When considering what to write, ask yourself, 'what
would the converse say about you'? No one is going to want to hire
someone that is lazy or an under-performer.
3. **Be truthful** – Do not tell the reader what they want to hear. This may get
you the interview but it will not win you the job.
4. **Avoiding being clichéd** – Attempt to use words that will make you stand
out from others.
5. **Keep it short** – Your profile statement should be a few sentences long,
each of which should be punchy and to the point.

If you have less than two years' work experience:

■ summarise your education and/or commercial/work experience;

- describe any specific or technical skills that are particularly relevant to your target position;
- elaborate on some of the skills you have gained or honed though studies and/or work experience;
- detail what drives you as a person and what you enjoy; and
- utilise personal attributes to express your personality and attitude towards work.

In summary, demonstrate enthusiasm, your ability to work as part of a team, your desire to work hard and achieve success.

If you have more than two years' work experience:

- provide an overview of your work experience and in which area and/or industry;
- present a summary of your achievements or detail one of your most impressive accomplishments;
- express your areas of expertise, elaborating on some of your core skills. Where apt provide a brief explanation of where or how these skills have been demonstrated;
- detail what drives you as a person and what you enjoy; and
- utilise personal attributes to express your personality and attitude towards work.

In summary, focus on skills, experience and achievements that are going to be particularly relevant to your target position.

EXAMPLES – LESS THAN TWO YEARS' WORK EXPERIENCE

*A self-confident **Economics Graduate** with a Master's Degree in Public Policy Economics. Currently conducting research at Warwick University in Policy Analysis and Economic Growth in Developing Economies. Recognised as focused, rational and open-minded with valuable work experience gained within developing countries. Driven by the desire to achieve significant results, displaying confidence, commitment and a positive 'can-do' attitude at all times.*

An enthusiastic individual with an impressive academic record and valuable experience of team supervision gained within a dynamic, customer service environment. Adopts a logical and analytical approach to business, is quick to grasp new ideas and has a proven ability to devise creative solutions to problems. Demonstrates the highest levels of organisation and prioritisation in order to meet tight deadlines, and possesses excellent interpersonal and people skills.

An ambitious and enterprising individual who enjoys being an integral part of or leading a team. Displays a strong commitment to deliver client value and is quick to grasp new ideas and concepts. Possesses excellent problem-solving and analytical capabilities, good networking skills and is able to communicate concisely at all levels. Highly motivated, enthusiastic and well organised with an innate ability to work well under pressure.

*A career driven, well-organised **graduate** with a Master's Degree in Insurance and Risk Management. Gained a solid understanding of Risk Management methods during studies and work experience, with a strong focus on various methods of controlling, identifying and financing risk. Displays well-defined analytical and numerical skills, a passion for finance and an ability to work well in a team and on own initiative. Demonstrates superb organising, leadership and planning capabilities coupled with an ability to communicate effectively at all levels.*

EXAMPLES – MORE THAN TWO YEARS' WORK EXPERIENCE

*A well-qualified **Childcare Practitioner** with seven years' experience working with children of varying ages. Highly committed to children's development and possesses a professional approach to managing and promoting positive children's behaviour. Displays an inborn ability to lead and motivate children and team members alike, and is recognised as kind, patient, loving and caring.*

*A highly analytical and self-motivated **Engineer** with a PhD in Mechanical Engineering and extensive experience of planning and managing several high-level research projects. Has developed expertise in rotational moulding and polymer processing and has a demonstrable record of using statistical analysis, mathematical modelling and computer simulation to improve and develop company processes. Resourceful and diplomatic with solid people management skills and an inborn ability to enthuse and motivate teams.*

*A methodical and highly enthusiastic **Prince2 qualified Project Manager** with over four years' progressive experience within the IT industry, specialising in infrastructure-based projects. Possesses a demonstrable track record of managing several award winning large-scale global projects worth up to £5m. Excellent delegation and influencing skills with a proven ability to consistently meet deadlines and effectively handle crisis situations. Motivated by challenge and thrives on high levels of autonomy and responsibility.*

*A **Creativity and Soft Skills Trainer** with an impressive track record of designing and presenting training modules that have significantly boosted company productivity. Proven leadership, interpersonal and communication skills substantiated by motivating over 4,000 individuals towards academic and professional success. Recognised as self-motivated and enthusiastic with a talent for generating new ideas and exceeding customer expectations.*

*A seasoned **Senior Manager** with expertise encompassing web and mobile technology underpinned by 10 years' progression with a leading telecommunications company. Accustomed to project managing high-profile projects and effectively co-ordinating resources to achieve targets within stringent time constraints. Relishes a challenge and demonstrates in-depth analytical and strategic ability to facilitate operational and procedural planning. Committed towards ongoing personal development as demonstrated by the recent completion of an MBA at Brunel University.*

*A well-respected **Finance Professional** with 10+ years Operational Finance and Internal Control experience gained within a blue-chip organisation. Possesses a proven track record of delivering business process re-engineering and positively impacting bottom-line profitability. An award winning leader in People Development, Diversity and Work-Life initiatives. Reputed as enthusiastic and results-driven; pays close attention to detail.*

EXAMPLES – CAREER CHANGERS

Seeking a role in Customer Service

A self-motivated individual with seven years' commercial experience gained in a variety of positions including marketing, administration and event management. Having worked in a variety of customer facing positions, is able to communicate effectively with people at all levels and has consistently been commended for exceeding customer expectations. Demonstrates strong multi-tasking and organisational skills, and displays an insatiable appetite for learning new skills and developing oneself. Thrives on working in fast-paced, demanding environments that reward hard work and determination.

Seeking a transition into Banking

An assertive, results-oriented professional with diverse experience across a variety of disciplines including sales, customer care and marketing. In possession of first-class customer focus, administration and negotiation skills as demonstrated by commendations received from clients, colleagues and management. A conscientious, people oriented individual who is adaptable to new working environments and gives one hundred percent at all times.

Seeking to secure a management position in a new industry

A motivated and profit driven Senior Manager with wide ranging experience in security, transport, leisure and construction industries.

A well-respected, disciplined leader with a natural ability to manage, motivate and inspire large teams of people under extreme conditions. Accustomed to identifying and implementing viable solutions to improve profitability and exceed company objectives. Displays integrity, loyalty and an enviable flair for business.

A teacher seeking to change career

An ambitious, dependable and highly confident teacher with over 20 years' experience working within a variety of educational and childcare environments. Extensive experience of promoting schools and nurseries, introducing and implementing new initiatives, fundraising and organising major events both internally and externally. More recently, as Head of Department, gained invaluable experience of motivating and supporting both staff and students. Well-organised, disciplined and efficient coupled with an innate ability to multi-task.

Seeking a senior role in business development

An intelligent and committed General Manager with 10 years' experience in the hospitality industry and more recently, recruitment. Thrives on working in fast-paced, challenging and highly sales-driven environments, and possesses a performance record of revitalising sales and entire departments to deliver consistent year-on-year growth for several companies. Energetic, focused, passionate and motivated with a reputation for developing and managing high-performance sales and management teams.

WRITING YOUR PROFILE STATEMENT

Now that you are armed with what to include and have several examples to draw upon, start working on your own career objective.

Begin by selecting a title. Titles include 'Profile', 'Profile Statement', 'Personal Profile', 'Personal Statement', 'Professional Profile' or 'Executive Summary'. The first four are more appropriate for those with less than two years' work experience; the latter for those with more than two years' work experience.

Below are three tables. The first is a list of personal attributes; the second, a list of key skills. Select four to five of the former, and three to four of the latter. The third table is a list of descriptive words that can be used to help construct your statement.

Table of personal attributes

Able	Dependable	Innovative	Punctual
Accurate	Decisive	Intelligent	Qualified
Adaptable	Detail-oriented	Inventive	Quick-thinking
Adventurous	Determined	Loyal	Rational
Alert	Diligent	Mature	Realist
Ambitious	Diplomatic	Methodical	Reliable
Articulate	Dynamic	Meticulous	Reputation
Assertive	Effective	Motivated	Resourceful
Astute	Efficient	Multilingual	Responsible
Attention to detail	Empathetic	Objective	Self-assured
Bilingual	Energetic	Observant	Self-confident
Bright	Enthusiastic	Open-minded	Self-motivated
Calm	Expertise	Organised	Self-reliant
Capable	Fast-track	Outgoing	Sensitive
Career-driven	Flexible	Passionate	Spirited
Caring	Focused	Patient	Successful
Clarity	Friendly	People-oriented	Supportive
Committed	Goal-driven	Perceptive	Talented
Competent	Good-humoured	Persistent	Tenacious
Confident	Hands-on	Personable	Thorough
Conscientious	Hardworking	Positive attitude	Thoughtful
Consistent	Helpful	Presentation	Time keeping
Co-operative	High-energy	Principled	Trustworthy
Creative	High-impact	Proactive	Understanding
Cross-functional	Honest	Productive	Versatile
Decisive	Imaginative	Professional	Willing
Dedicated	Independent	Proficient	

Table of skills

Administration	Motivating	Public speaking
Analysing	Multi-tasking	Relationship building
Communicating	Negotiating	Results-oriented

Crisis resolution	Numerate	Start-ups
Customer focus	Operating	Strategising
Decision-making	Organising	Team leader
Delegating	Planning	Team player
Interpersonal	Presenting	Technical
Lateral thinking	Problem-solving	Track record
Leading	Profit-driving	Trouble-shooting
Managing	Project management	

Table of descriptive words

Able	Developed	Instils	Skilled
Accomplished	Displays	Natural	Solid
Accustomed to	Engenders	Outstanding	Strong
Acquired	Equipped	Participated	Superb
Adept	Established	Possesses	Superior
Awarded	Exceptional	Practised	Talented
Boasts	Exhibits	Recognised	Trained
Broad	Extensive	Refined	Well-defined
Capable	Gained	Regarded	Well-respected
Delivers	Honed	Renowned	Wide-ranging
Demonstrated	In-depth	Reputed	

Tip

Should you not utilise all of the skills that you selected when you construct your profile, the additional ones can be incorporated into the next section, Key Skills.

For more inspiration, refer to the appended CD.

CHAPTER 9

KEY SKILLS

The next step after your profile is to detail your key skills or areas of expertise. This chapter will help you identify and compile your core skills and strengths, and in the case of a functional CV, your transferable skills most relevant to your target position.

A skill is defined as, *'the ability, coming from one's knowledge, practice, aptitude etc., to perform an activity very well.'*

A transferable skill is defined as, *'skills and knowledge gained throughout your life whether it be during employment, sport, parenting, hobbies etc., that are then applicable and transferable to what you do in your next job.'*

BENEFITS OF A KEY SKILLS SECTION

This section provides you with an opportunity to quickly express your suitability to a role and/or show a prospective employer what skills you will bring to their business. Organisations are increasingly using software to pre-screen CVs. Additionally, recruitment professionals screening your CV will be actively seeking out your skills to ensure that you are a good match for the role in question, so having a separate key skills section will ensure they **JUMP** out.

Unless you have included all of your key skills in your profile statement, as may be the case for more junior level CVs, it is recommended that you include this section.

IDENTIFYING YOUR KEY SKILLS OR AREAS OF EXPERTISE

For new entrants, i.e. those with less than two years' work experience, consider skills that may have been gained during studies, an internship, a work placement, voluntary work or part-time jobs.

For those with more than two years' work experience, give some serious thought to what core skills or transferable skills you have gained during your career.

Below are two tables detailing both soft and technical skills. These lists are not exhaustive and are to be used as a guideline only.

Soft skills

Administration	Analysing	Communicating
Crisis resolution	Customer focus	Decision-making
Delegating	Interpersonal	Lateral thinking
Leading	Managing	Motivating
Multi-tasking	Negotiating	Numerate
Operating	Organising	Planning
Presenting	Problem-solving	Profit-driving
Project management	Public speaking	Relationship building
Results-oriented	Start-ups	Strategising
Team leader	Team player	Technical
Trouble-shooting		

Business/technical skills

Account management	Administration	Advertising
Business development	Change management	Communication
Communications	Construction	Consulting
Counselling	Designing	Editing
Electronics	Engineering	Financial management
Human resources	Insurance	Journalism
Law	Management	Marketing
Organisation	Planning	Production
Project management	Promotion	Public relations
Publishing	Research	Sales
Start-ups	Strategic planning	Training
Travel	Writing	

Determine which skills to highlight

Include those skills that will be most relevant to your target position. These skills could be skills that you have gained during your career or through voluntary work, and for those with less than two years' work experience, skills gained whilst at university, school or college.

Should you be looking to apply for roles where you have little or no experience, identify your transferable skills.

If you have been with one company or in the same type of job for several years and you are looking to do a similar role in the same or in a different industry, focus on the core skills that you have honed or developed over the years.

Should you be uncertain about what jobs may be suitable at this stage, merely list all of your core skills. When you find a job that particularly interests you, amend the order in which you present your skills, presenting the most important skills first, and remove any that are not relevant.

Below are ways to establish which skills you should be highlighting:

1. **If you are responding to a specific position:** Gather information from the job advertisement, job description, and/or person specification to establish what skills they specify as 'must have' and 'nice to have'.

   If the skills required are radically different to your own, rethink whether the job is a viable opportunity.

2. **If you are applying speculatively:** Research the company website to determine what skills and attributes they look for in an employee. Read through job advertisements of similar roles to establish what skills they typically require.

3. **Other ways to determine your strengths:** Speak with colleagues, peers and friends. Review old performance appraisals. Both these methods can be quite enlightening and may identify skills you take for granted.

> **Tip**
>
> **Besides listing your skills that match the job requirements, consider including others skills that may be supportive to your application or would be an added benefit to a prospective employer.**

EXAMPLES OF KEY SKILLS

Example 1: Graduate

- Leadership
- Team player
- Administration
- Customer focus
- Research
- Organisation and prioritisation

Example 2: Accountant

- Reporting
- Risk management
- Relationship management
- IT skills
- Trouble-shooting
- Analysis

Example 3: Sales Professional

- Account management
- Business development
- People management
- Negotiating
- Networking

Example 4: Business Consultant

- Service management
- Project management
- Training and development
- Business development
- Marketing
- Strategic design

With the above in mind, write down up to seven skills that best describe you and are most appropriate to your target position, with a minimum of three.

r – **Tip** –

Be careful not to repeat skills already mentioned in your profile statement. Repetition reduces the impact of your CV.

Should you have more than seven skills, you can opt for two separate sections: one entitled 'Key Skills' and the other 'Area of Expertise'. The former would need to be your soft skills and the latter your more technical skills. Having two sections would be more appropriate for senior executives or those working in a niche sector.

COMPILING YOUR KEY SKILLS SECTION

This section can be entitled 'Key Skills' or 'Key Strengths' in more junior CVs or 'Key Words', 'Major Competencies', 'Key Skills' or 'Areas of Expertise' in more senior level CVs.

How much detail, if any, you provide under each skill will depend on the CV type you have selected. Each CV type will be discussed separately.

1. Chronological CVs

With a chronological CV you will be looking to highlight anywhere from three to seven core skills. The information can be presented in two ways: as 'Buzz Words' or as 'Statements'.

(a) Buzz words

Here, merely list buzz words or key words that describe your strengths or areas of expertise.

EXAMPLE – LESS THAN TWO YEARS' WORK EXPERIENCE

Example 1: Target Position – Administrator

- *Communicating and interpersonal*
- *Organising and planning*
- *Team player*
- *Time management*

Example 2: Target Position – Financial Analyst

- *Research and analytical*
- *Lateral thinking*
- *Presenting*
- *Mathematical modelling*
- *Multi-tasking*

EXAMPLES – MORE THAN TWO YEARS' WORK EXPERIENCE

Example 1: Call Centre Manager/Team Leader

- *Customer service*
- *Organisation and planning*
- *Interpersonal and communication*
- *Conflict resolution*
- *Team management*
- *Full project life-cycle management*

Example 2: Financial Accountant

- *Budgetary control*
- *Financial management*
- *Forecasting*
- *P&L*
- *People management*
- *Project management*
- *Strategic planning*

Example 3: Change Manager

- *Change management*
- *Crisis management*
- *Customer focus*
- *Product development*
- *Six sigma*
- *Strategic planning*
- *Training*

> **Tip**
>
> You can include both your technical and soft skills; 'Buzz Words' may be used to describe industry specific skills and 'Statements', to express your soft skills. As mentioned in the previous hint, you can then have two separate sections to describe your skills. It would look like Example 4 below.

Example 4: Change Manager

Areas of expertise
- *Change management*
- *Crisis resolution*
- *Business re-engineering*
- *Product development*
- *Six sigma*
- *Strategic planning*

Key skills
- **Communicating** – *Exhibits strong communication skills, both written and verbal, and is adept at communicating effectively with people at all levels.*
- **Leadership** – *Proficient with leading, mentoring and motivating multi-disciplined teams.*
- **Organising** – *Successfully co-ordinated and planned several corporate events for up to 500 people.*
- **Presenting** – *An accomplished presenter with experience of delivering seminars and training audiences of 1,000+, both in the UK and abroad.*
- **Training** – *Extensive experience of delivering one-to-one coaching and training sessions, on both technical and customer service requirements, to all areas of the business.*

(b) Statements
Should you opt for the 'Statement' approach, give some thought to how each skill was gained, learned or demonstrated. Be as specific as possible and

where appropriate, provide evidence of where a skill has been demonstrated or how you have honed or learnt a skill.

EXAMPLES – LESS THAN TWO YEARS' WORK EXPERIENCE

Example 1:

- *Strong team player who works well in a team and on own initiative*
- *Excellent organisational and planning skills developed whilst completing various assignments within tight timescales*
- *Responsible and reliable with first-class time management skills as demonstrated by . . .*
- *An insatiable appetite for learning and developing oneself*

Example 2:

- *Thrives under pressure, displaying initiative and flexibility*
- *Exceptionally thorough with an unwillingness to compromise on quality or standards*
- *Adept at quickly absorbing knowledge and retaining information*
- *Skilled at accurately interpreting financial information*

Example 3:

- ***Communicating*** *– A talent for establishing rapport and engendering trust with clients and colleagues.*
- ***Customer Service*** *– Developed an ability to understand customer needs and enhance a customer's experience, through working in a variety of customer centric positions.*
- ***Leadership*** *– Developed team leadership skills from an early age, having been elected as a Prefect at both primary and senior school.*
- ***Computer Skills*** *– Fully conversant with Microsoft Office, Sage 50 and Dreamweaver.*

Example 4:

- **Leadership** – Developed team leading skills whilst working as a <job title> for <company name> and whilst leading group study activities at university.
- **Presenting** – Accustomed to present effectively and confidently to small groups of students and lecturers.
- **Interpersonal** – As a result of outstanding interpersonal skills is able to easily develop solid working relationships with colleagues and clients.
- **Team Player** – A natural team player who is able to encourage and enthuse others in order to meet objectives and goals.
- **Research** – Extensive experience of preparing and compiling research documents for university projects and as part of internship.

Example 5:

- **Financial Analysis** – Completed several research projects during studies, which involved the detailed analysis of company financials, share price and dividend policy.
- **Project Management** – Successfully demonstrated project skills by <provide an example>.
- **Report Writing** – Experience of preparing several essays and papers in a methodical and organised manner during degree course.
- **Research** – Accustomed to performing detailed research using a variety of methods and sources, including literature, the internet and media.

Example 6: Event Manager/PR Manager

- **Event Management** – Solid experience of arranging and co-ordinating several high-profile corporate events.
- **Marketing/PR** – Gained experience in sales, marketing and PR with particular reference to . . .
- **Project Management** – Experienced with co-ordinating projects from inception through to completion as confirmed when . . .
- **Planning** – Extensive experience of organising and prioritising workload, often completing tasks ahead of schedule.

Tip

It is not imperative to include a 'Key Skills' section if it means you are going to be repeating information from your profile.

Should you have no work experience, it is recommended that you produce a key skills section and draw upon skills gained or learned during your studies.

EXAMPLES – MORE THAN TWO YEARS' WORK EXPERIENCE

Example 1: Store Manager

- *A methodical, open and flexible approach to business, developed through a background in retail and customer service.*
- *Exceptionally people oriented with a management style that empowers and motivates teams to achieve both company and personal objectives.*
- *Full P&L responsibility with experience of controlling budgets of up to £1m.*
- *Experience of devising and developing corporate strategies to achieve growth and profitability.*

Example 2: Operations Manager

- *An accomplished and well-respected man-manager with extensive experience of leading, inspiring and motivating multi-cultural teams of up to 30 people.*
- *A talent for implementing new systems and processes to reduce costs, thereby maximising savings.*
- *Skilled at formulating recommendations and policy options to effectively tackle both regional and national challenges.*
- *A logical thinker who exhibits the ability to resolve complex problems quickly and efficiently.*
- *Extensive experience of restructuring departments in order to deliver improved services and provide scope for expansion.*

Example 3: Sales Executive

- *Adept at building and developing solid working relationships with clients and suppliers.*
- *Possesses a consultative selling approach, which resulted in many referrals and repeat business.*
- *Well-honed negotiation and influencing skills as demonstrated by the consistent ability to meet and often exceed targets.*
- *Practised in maintaining accounting records and managing budgets of up to £0.5m.*
- *Confident decision-maker, able to make commercial decisions based upon an impressive knowledge of the industry.*
- *Dedicated team player who works well in a team and on own initiative.*

Example 4: Marketing Professional

- ***Communicating** – Exhibits strong communication skills, both written and verbal, and is adept at communicating effectively with people at all levels.*
- ***Change Management** – A proven ability to effectively manage change to enhance efficiency within an organisation.*
- ***Marketing** – In-depth knowledge of product marketing and branding, including launching, selling and positioning products.*
- ***Business Development** – Accustomed to defining a target market, formulating effective marketing strategies and identifying new business opportunities in order to positively impact bottom-line profitability.*
- ***Leadership** – Proficient with leading, mentoring and motivating multi-disciplined teams.*
- ***Organising** – Successfully co-ordinated and planned several corporate events for up to 500 people.*

Example 5: Office Manager

- ***Administration** – Experienced with maintaining up-to-date, accurate records, and analysing and providing recommendations on various development reports.*

- **Planning** – Demonstrable ability of prioritising and scheduling tasks effectively, delegating responsibility where necessary.
- **Relationship Building** – Skilled at building long-standing customer relationships through engendering trust and displaying absolute integrity throughout all business transactions.
- **Computer Skills** – Advanced Microsoft Office, with keyboard skills of 65 words per minute.
- **Organising** – Experienced with managing the day-to-day operations of the office including monitoring stock levels and maintaining office equipment.

Example 6: General Manager

- **People Management** – A seasoned manager with experience of leading, motivating and providing direction to multi-cultural teams of up to 15 people.
- **Operations** – Adept at managing the day-to-day operations of a business and implementing systems and processes that have saved the company both time and money.
- **Presenting** – An accomplished presenter with experience of delivering seminars and training audiences of 1,000+, both in the UK and abroad.
- **Strategic Development** – Skilled at creating, implementing and managing short, medium and long-term plans to instigate and maintain product growth and creation.
- **Training** – Extensive experience of delivering one-to-one coaching and training sessions, on both technical and customer service requirements, to all areas of the business.

Example 7:

A **Design Engineer** may have industry specific skills such as:

- 3D
- CAD
- FEM 3D Analysis

A **Clinical Psychologist** may wish to highlight their skills in:

- *Psychological assessment*
- *Counselling*
- *Systematic therapies*

A **Journalist** would want to highlight their:

- *Writing*
- *Subbing*
- *Public relations*

An **Investment Banker** may want to highlight their experience with:

- *Trend and competitor analysis*
- *Portfolio management*
- *Revenue and asset management*

Each one of these can then be listed as buzz words or expanded upon.

2. Chrono-functional CVs

If you have opted for a chrono-functional CV, you should have anywhere from three to seven skills, and you will be looking to provide two/three points per skill. This section would take up around half a page.

List skills in order of importance. The order will need to be changed each time you send out your application and will depend on the requirements of the role.

Under each of the skills you have selected provide a demonstrable example/ achievement or summarise your experience. The more specific you can be, the better.

EXAMPLES – LESS THAN TWO YEARS' WORK EXPERIENCE

Example 1: Team Leader – Call Centre

Organising
- Proven ability to prioritise, schedule and co-ordinate workload as demonstrated whilst . . .
- As a result of strong leadership skills, is able to effectively organise workload among individuals and utilise the personal strengths of individuals to maximise results.

People Management
- Natural ability to lead, motivate and manage small teams as demonstrated during the completion of . . .
- Able to direct a team and delegate tasks in order to perform tasks effectively.

Presenting
- An accomplished presenter having prepared and conducted several school and work presentations to audiences of up to 30 people.
- Gained good presentation skills through project work at university and through former role as a . . .

Problem Solving
- A logical and lateral thinker able to act quickly and efficiently to resolve complex problems.
- Commended by colleagues for utilising initiative to resolve complex problems.

Relationship Building
- As a result of outstanding interpersonal skills is able to easily develop solid working relationships with colleagues and clients
- Adept at forging strong relationships with peers and clients alike.

Team Player
- Developed strong team working skills through managing and participating in several team assignments and projects at school, university and throughout work placements.
- Works equally well on own initiative or leading a team.

Example 2: Accountant

Accounting

- Completed several research projects during studies, which involved the detailed analysis of company financials, share price and dividend policy.
- Accustomed to using financial models such as . . . and . . .
- Gained a good understanding of accounting principles through studies and relevant work experience.

Project Management

- Successfully demonstrated project skills by <provide an example>.
- Demonstrable record of delivering high quality projects on time and to budget.
- Experienced with successfully planning and managing challenging assignments within agreed timescales.

Report Writing

- Experience of preparing several essays and papers in a methodical and organised manner during degree course.
- Highly developed report writing skills for both technical and non-technical audiences.

Customer Service

- Consistently commended by customers for being supportive, helpful and for exceeding their expectations.
- Exceptionally committed to providing superior levels of customer service as displayed in all part-time positions.

Example 3: PA

Administration

- Highly organised with good planning and time management skills.
- Adept at maintaining accurate records as demonstrated as a data entry clerk.

Communicating

- Possesses excellent communication skills, written and verbal, and is equipped to communicate effectively at all levels.
- Through various part-time roles, honed the ability to engage and build rapport with a wide range of people.

Computer/Technical skills

- Highly computer literate with a strong technical understanding of various programmes and systems including Microsoft Office and Sage.
- Impressive keyboard skills at 80 wpm, coupled with a high level of accuracy.

Customer Service

- Consistently commended by customers for being supportive, helpful and for exceeding their expectations.
- Exceptionally committed to providing superior levels of customer service as displayed in all part-time positions.

EXAMPLES – MORE THAN TWO YEARS' WORK EXPERIENCE

Example 1: Customer Service Executive

Customer Focus

- A good listener who is skilled at identifying customer requirements and providing solutions to meet their individual needs.
- Maintains regular communication with key accounts and supports the sales process, deputising in the absence of the sales manager.

Communication

- Cultivated a talent for communicating effectively with people from diverse cultures and backgrounds through working at a variety of multi-nationals.
- Practised at effectively dealing with and resolving complaints from difficult, demanding customers.

Relationship Building

- *Adept at engaging with and forging long-standing relationships with customers and colleagues alike.*
- *Engenders trust with customers by displaying absolute integrity in all business transactions.*

Example 2: Sales Manager

Business Development/Sales

- *Attended monthly networking events and seminars that significantly increased the visibility and profile of company XYZ.*
- *Accustomed to defining a target market, formulating effective marketing strategies and identifying new business opportunities in order to positively impact bottom-line profitability.*

Training

- *In collaboration with senior management, identified training needs and development plans for all sales personnel across the whole of the UK.*
- *Developed the content for a training manual at XYZ company that is still being utilised today.*
- *Experience of delivering one-to-one coaching and training sessions, on both technical and customer service requirements, to all areas of the business.*

Communicating/Presenting

- *Exhibits strong communication skills, both written and verbal, and is adept with communicating effectively with people at all levels.*
- *An accomplished presenter who is able to present information clearly and is skilled with engaging an audience.*
- *Liaise daily with suppliers and customers to ensure the smooth delivery of goods and services.*

3. Functional CVs

The skills section of a functional CV will form the focus of your CV, and as a consequence, you will need to expend a lot of time here. You should have anywhere from three to seven skills, and you will be looking to provide a minimum of two points per skill and a maximum of four/five. This section will take up almost a full page.

List skills in order of importance. The order will need to be changed each time you send out your CV and will depend on the requirements of the role.

Under each skill, provide a demonstrable example/achievement or summarise your overall experience. The more specific you can be, the better. The examples you provide can relate to any aspect of your life, whether it be a skill gained through a sporting interest, a project managed or voluntary work, as long as it is relevant to your target position. Attempt to provide examples that are fairly current, i.e. within the last five years; it is however, acceptable to draw upon early experiences.

Record details of the company you worked for, the role you were in or the specific year involved. Or merely state the fact.

Example 1:

A person seeking a role in Customer Service may look to highlight Communication, Relationship Building, Customer Focus and perhaps Administration skills.

Customer Focus

- *A good listener who is skilled at identifying customer requirements and providing solutions to meet their individual needs.*
- *Maintains regular communication with key accounts and supports the sales process, deputising in the absence of the sales manager.*

Communication

- *Cultivated a talent to communicate effectively with people from diverse cultures and backgrounds through working at a variety of multi-nationals.*
- *Practised at effectively dealing with and resolving complaints from difficult, demanding customers.*

Relationship Building

- *Adept at engaging with and forging long-standing relationships with customers and colleagues alike.*
- *Engenders trust with customers by displaying absolute integrity in all business transactions.*

Administration

- *Managed the stationery requirements and equipment maintenance for a busy office of up to 40 staff.*
- *Designed and implemented a new system that improved the accuracy of client records.*
- *In-depth experience of minute taking, diary management and handling correspondence.*

Example 2:

An individual with diverse experience seeking to secure a position in sales may wish to emphasise very similar skills to the above but may include 'Business Development/Sales', and also change the order in which the skills are presented.

Business Development/Sales

- *As a telemarketer, acquired 20 new accounts within the first month of joining and was acknowledged as 'Employee of the Month'.*
- *Attended monthly networking events and seminars that significantly increased the visibility and profile of company XYZ.*
- *Accustomed to defining a target market, formulating effective marketing strategies and identifying new business opportunities in order to positively impact bottom-line profitability.*

Customer Focus

- *Maintains regular communication with key accounts and supports the sales process, deputising in the absence of the sales manager.*
- *A good listener who is skilled at identifying customer requirements and providing solutions to meet their individual needs.*

Communication

- *Practised at effectively dealing with and resolving complaints from difficult, demanding customers.*
- *Cultivated a talent to communicate effectively with people from diverse cultures and backgrounds through working at a variety of multi-nationals.*

Relationship Building

- *Adept at engaging with and forging long-standing relationships with customers and colleagues alike.*
- *Engenders trust with customers by displaying absolute integrity in all business transactions.*

An individual seeking to secure a position as a Relationship Manager in the Banking sector or perhaps a Search Consultant in the Recruitment industry could again select very similar skills to the ones mentioned in Example 2.

Example 3:

In this example, the individual is looking to draw upon vast experience gained in a variety of roles across a number of industries to secure a training role in the public sector.

Training

- *Prepared and delivered several in-house training programmes to hotel staff.*
- *In collaboration with senior management, identified training needs and development plans for their individual teams.*
- *Developed the content for a training manual at XYZ company that is still being utilised today.*
- *Experience of delivering one-to-one coaching and training sessions, on both technical and customer service requirements, to all areas of the business.*

Communication/Presentation

- *Exhibits strong communication skills, both written and verbal, and is adept at communicating effectively with people at all levels.*
- *An accomplished presenter who is able to present information clearly and is skilled with engaging an audience.*
- *Liaise daily with suppliers and customers to ensure the smooth delivery of goods and services.*

Organisation/Planning

- *Adept at maintaining accurate staff records for 300+ employees.*
- *Managed an office relocation project that involved moving and re-housing 200 staff and all office equipment.*
- *Demonstrable ability of prioritising and scheduling tasks effectively, delegating responsibility where necessary.*
- *Successfully co-ordinated and planned several corporate events for up to 500 people.*

Relationship Management

- *Skilled with developing and maintaining good working relationships with internal and external customers.*
- *Forges strong relationships with key players in the industry, developing mutually beneficial relationships that result in objectives being surpassed.*

Management

- *A natural leader with experience of managing and motivating teams of up to 10 staff.*
- *Reputed to provide direction to and develop multi-cultural teams.*

Computer Literacy

- *Fully conversant with Microsoft Office, including PowerPoint, Word and Publisher.*
- *Good understanding of various design packages including Photoshop.*

SUMMARY

This section should be tweaked depending on the role being applied for. Simply change the order in which you present the skills, presenting them in order of importance and add/remove certain skills depending on what is required. The key is to make your CV as targeted as possible and this is definitely one of the areas where this can be achieved.

Use the descriptive words provided in Chapter 8 and at the end of the book to produce your key skills section.

If you feel that your profile adequately sums up all your skills and you feel you have no further skills or strengths to add (which may often be the case in more junior level CVs), do not feel pressurised to include this section, particularly if it means that you are likely to repeat information from your profile statement.

For more examples, refer to the appended CD.

CHAPTER 10

EDUCATIONAL BACKGROUND

The next step in the process is to detail your education, qualifications, professional development and training. This section needs to detail your highest level of attainment and work backwards.

The amount of detail that needs to be provided and the amount of time you need to dedicate to this section will depend on how much work experience you have.

CANDIDATES WITH LESS THAN TWO YEARS' EXPERIENCE

As an entry-level job seeker, your educational history is going to be of most interest to a prospective employer and hence, it must form the focus of your CV. In essence, this section should take up around half a page and it needs to be very detailed and thorough.

Detailing your education

Your educational history must be listed in reverse chronological order, i.e. most recent first. Provide the name of the qualification, the institution, the dates you commenced, completed or expect to complete your studies.

This section can be entitled 'Education', 'Education and Qualifications', or 'Education and Training'. It can also be split into 'Education' and 'Professional Development', or kept all under one heading.

1. Degrees

Provide the name of the degree, to what level (honours), any dissertations or final year projects, followed by core subjects/modules and grade. Where top grades have been achieved in a particular subject, insert the details. Degrees should be abbreviated, for example, Bachelor of Science should be written as BSc.

Example 1:

BSc in Economics, York University: 2:1   *2003–2006*

Dissertation: *'An analysis of . . .'*
Core Modules: *Microeconomics, Macroeconomics,*
                      Econometrics and Quantitative Techniques

Example 2:

Queen Mary College, University of London:

2007–Date   *MSc in Chemical Process Engineering*
                  Core Modules: Process Dynamic & Control, Fluid Particle
                  Systems, Safety & Loss Prevention

2004–2007   *BSc (Hons) in Chemical Engineering: 1st Class*
                  Core Modules: Process Dynamics, Environmental
                  Engineering, Heat Transfer Operation

2. Diplomas and college education

Provide details of the grade you achieved, i.e. pass, merit, credit or level
achieved, and the modules or subjects completed. Where top grades have
been achieved in a particular subject, insert the details. Diplomas should be
abbreviated, for example BTEC National Diploma.

Example 1:

HND, West London University: 72%   *2005–2006*

Example 2:

ABC College of Further Education:

BTEC National Diploma in Engineering – Merit	*2007–2008*
BTEC First Diploma in Engineering – Merit	*2006–2007*
NVC, Engineering Assembly Level 1	*2005–2006*

3. Courses and certifications

Provide details of the course or certification, the name of the institution and the year awarded.

Example 1:

NCFE Certificate, Computer Technology, 2007
City & Guilds Certificate, Computer Aided Design, 2006

Example 2:

2001	*Community Sports Leadership Award (CSLA)*
2000	*First Aid Course*

4. School education

Provide details of the number of 'A' levels, 'AS' Levels, GCSEs or Scottish Highers attained; summarise your GCSEs. For higher qualifications furnish more detail including subjects and grade.

Example 1:

3 'A' Levels, St Mary's School for Girls   *2004–2006*
Subjects: English (A), Mathematics (B), Business Studies (B)

8 GCSEs grades A–C including Mathematics and English *1999–2004*

Example 2:

4 'A' Levels, XYZ College, Southampton   2001–2003
Physics (B), Economics (B), General Studies (C), Biology (B)

9 GCSEs, XYZ School, Romsey   1996–2001
Grades A–B including Mathematics, English and Science

Tip

**Academics who have spent many years studying may find it necessary
to include an Appendix, i.e. a separate page detailing qualifications and
professional development.**

CANDIDATES WITH MORE THAN TWO YEARS' EXPERIENCE

At this level, your career history is going to be of more interest to a prospective
employer. Consequently, this section need not be very detailed.

Detailing your education

Select an appropriate heading: 'Education', 'Education and Qualifications',
'Education and Professional Development', 'Education and Training', or
'Education and Certifications'.

It is here that you would highlight your education and qualifications, and list any
special courses passed, certifications received or seminars attended.

Your educational history should be listed in reverse chronological order, i.e.
most recent first. Provide the name of the qualification, the institution, the
dates you completed or expect to complete your studies.

Example 1:

MBA, *Heriot-Watt University, Edinburgh*	*2001*
BSc (Hons) Elec Eng *with Computer Science, UCT*	*1992*
Certificate in Quantitative Finance, *7city, London*	*Ongoing*
Mathematics for Quantitative Finance, *7city, London*	*2006*

Example 2:

BA (Hons) Degree in Business Studies, *Warwick University, 1995*
HND in Business & Finance, *Kingston College, 1993*

Example 3:

Various in-house courses including:

Basic Food Hygiene & Employee Relationship Course	*2005*
First Aid Certificate	*2003*
Two 'O' Levels	*2002*

Example 4:

1998 BTEC Foundation course in Art and Design
1996 Two 'A' Levels in Art and General Studies
1994 Six GCSEs including Mathematics and English

Example 5:

BENG (Hons) in Telecommunications, University of Essex	*2005*

Certifications:

MSTC Microsoft Windows Mobile 5.0: Configuration	*2003*
MCSE Windows Server	*2003*

Courses:
Leadership Programme, in-house
Presentation Skills, in-house

- Include the name of the qualification, the institution where you studied and the date/expected date of completion.
- It is only necessary to include the date that you completed the qualification, not the date you commenced the qualification.
- Do not provide grades unless you achieved a first degree, straight As or something extraordinary.
- Do not include the names of subjects or dissertations unless you believe it is truly relevant.
- If you have a degree, it is not necessary to provide details of schooling.
- It is not necessary to include the name of where you went to school.
- Include only courses, certifications or seminars attended if relevant to your target position.
- Separate professional qualifications from courses, and list them from highest level of attainment to lowest.
- Abbreviate degrees and course names.

OBSTACLES YOU MAY FACE

■ Poor grades

It is important not to include or draw attention to anything negative on a CV, and as such, it is recommended that any grades below average be omitted.

For those with over two years' experience, grades need not be provided.

■ No real education to speak of

Employers are interested in your highest level of attainment and as such include this section even if you have just one GCSE. If you did not complete school, include any courses attended.

■ You have completed many courses

If you are focused on professional development, you may struggle to include all your courses on your CV without exceeding the page limit. Consider listing only those that are relevant to your target position. If you are an academic or all your courses are relevant, include an appendix.

■ **Incomplete qualification**

Perhaps you enrolled on a course or began studying towards a degree or diploma that you were ill suited for or visa versa. It may be possible to omit it from you CV. Why draw attention to something or line yourself up for uncomfortable interview questions if you can avoid it. If, however, it results in an obvious gap you will need to include the qualification. Put in brackets (incomplete) or if relevant to what you are applying for, include the details of subjects passed.

■ **Your qualification is ongoing**

If you are still studying, simply state as 'ongoing', or express as 200X–Date, or state expected completion date.

■ **Education completed abroad**

Job seekers from abroad are habitually looking to work and practise in the area for which they have been trained. As such, it may be necessary to convert your qualifications to the UK equivalent. This can be achieved by contacting one of the following national agencies below. This is particularly important if you require a certain qualification or grade in order to apply for the role.

UK Naric – Official provider of information on international qualifications for over 180 countries (www.naric.org.uk).

UK NRP – Evaluate international vocational qualifications (www.uknrp.org. uk).

■ **Poor command of the English language**

For many jobseekers coming from abroad, English may not be their first language. Completing the IELTS or the TOEIC tests will make you more marketable.

1. The IELTS (International English Language Testing System)
This testing system assesses language abilities and tests listening, reading, writing and speaking capabilities.

IELTS is jointly managed by:

- University of Cambridge ESOL Examinations;
- British Council;
- IDP Education Australia: IELTS Australia.

There are many practice exams that can be completed online and many test centres across the UK, most of which are colleges and universities.

The global website is: www.ielts.org.

2. TOEIC (Test of English for International Communication)

This test is designed to evaluate the listening and reading skills of non-native speakers who need to use English in the workplace and is administered as open public sessions, and at companies and language schools around the world.

TOEIC was developed and is administered by ETS, a US-based, non-profit institution. The test is widely accepted by corporations, English language programs, and government agencies around the world.

As with IELTS, you can undertake online preparation courses. Tests take place at various language centres across the UK.

WHERE TO POSITION EDUCATIONAL BACKGROUND

Where to place this section is dependent on how well your education enhances your application.

If your education is your strongest selling point, as will be for those with less than two years' experience or those who have recently completed or are close to completing a qualification that is a prerequisite for your target position, this section should be placed directly after key skills. In the absence of a key skills section, your education should come directly after your profile.

> *For some candidates, particularly in the university market, in some ways the most immediately impressive thing about their profile will probably be their educational record and their educational background. For that reason it's important in my mind that that's almost the first thing that greets the eye on the page.*
>
> Jonathan Jones at Goldman Sachs

If your work experience is stronger, as will be for the majority of people with more than two years' work experience, this section should feature directly after employment history.

Tip

If when applying for a role, it is imperative that you have a particular qualification, draw attention to this on the first page of your CV. Either include the letters after your name, highlight the qualification in your profile or present your education on page one of your CV.

Spend some time detailing your educational history. For more examples refer to the appended CD.

CHAPTER 11

ACHIEVEMENTS

An achievement is defined as *'something accomplished successfully, especially by means of exertion, skill, practice or perseverance'.*

An achievement is unique to your experience and is your opportunity to provide evidence of your capabilities. Demonstrating what you have achieved in the past provides a prospective employer with a good insight into what you are capable of achieving in the future.

> ❝ *77% of HR professionals expressed that a summary of achievements on page one of your CV is a useful addition.* ❞
>
> CMC Survey 2007

Most of us are really poor when it comes to selling ourselves. As such, this section can be the most difficult to write. Generally, people do not want to brag or 'blow their own trumpet', but this section can give you the edge; it can help you stand out. The important thing to note when compiling this section is to remain humble – prospective employers find arrogance offensive.

The next few pages provide a step-by-step process on how to identify and express achievements. Numerous examples are provided, and the chapter also covers difficulties that you may face.

CANDIDATES WITH LESS THAN TWO YEARS' WORK EXPERIENCE

As a first time job seeker, you have very little experience to draw on. Consequently, it is important to highlight any specific duties or responsibilities undertaken at school, college or university. Include anything that will show your future employer that you will be useful to them in the workplace.

Detailing leadership capabilities and achievements

1. Leadership roles

To demonstrate to a prospective employer what you have accomplished in the past and what you are capable of, furnish examples of any leadership roles undertaken at school, college or university. These can include appointments as a prefect, student representative or captain of a team through to leading group discussions or founding societies.

Examples:

Appointed as Head Prefect at XYZ high school.

Co-founded a Chinese society at XYZ university. Organised several social events and provided help to students experiencing cultural difficulties.

As Student Representative, worked closely with lecturers and students to resolve course work problems.

Elected as Chairman of XYZ committee whilst at university.

Appointed president of the Divers' Club for two consecutive years whilst at University.

Captained the cricket and hockey teams of XYZ school in 2001 and 2002.

Led group discussions for final year project at XYZ university.

Give some serious thought to where you may have demonstrated leadership capabilities and write down your examples. Incorporate details of your role, when it occurred and what your involvement was (where appropriate). Should you have no examples, this section should be omitted from your CV.

2. Achievements

As mentioned earlier, this is a great opportunity to show an employer where you have shone and provides them with an insight into what you are capable of.

So, how do you determine what your achievements are? Review school reports or appraisals received during work experience; speak with your parents, friends, colleagues and peers.

Achievements can be in the form of commendations, awards received, academic achievements, scholarships or sporting triumphs. Essentially, include anything that you have been particularly proud of.

Consider what your achievements have been and take the time to write these down. As with leadership examples, provide details of your actions and wherever possible, quantify. Ideally, try to include between two and five achievements. Should you have no examples, this section should be omitted from your CV.

Examples:

Received a special award from the Head of the English department in recognition of . . .

Achieved 75% for a final year project that involved writing a paper about . . .

Organised a highly successful university fresher party which attracted over 1,000 students.

Achieved distinctions in Corporate Finance and Control Systems in final year of Master's degree.

Won first prize in high school for . . .

Crowned chess champion for three consecutive years whilst at school.

A committed member of the hockey, tennis and athletics teams throughout school and university.

Won two regional awards as Director of the Young Enterprise group.

Received the Bronze Duke of Edinburgh award.

Attained the History prize for the highest grade in school.

Awarded a full Scholarship from XYZ University from 2000 to 2003.

Introduced and developed an intranet for a PR company, which reduced the number of time-consuming administration duties.

Joined XYZ Ltd as a weekend Sales Advisor, and was promoted to Footwear Supervisor three months later.

Actively promoted the XYZ charity via outgoing telephone calls to donors; raised an average of £1,500 per month on a part-time basis.

Devised and introduced a new spreadsheet that accurately recorded data and was easily accessible and logical to all staff. The system was so successful that it replaced the previous one that had been in operation for over 10 years.

Tip

These points can be expressed as sub-headings under the title of Education. If they relate to a mixture of schooling and work experience examples, express as a separate section below Education or include some under the sub-heading of education and the work experience examples under work experience.

Obstacles you may face

■ **Too few achievements**

Combine them with leadership roles, or if they are work related, highlight them under work experience.

■ **No achievements or leadership examples to speak of**

Not everyone is an academic, a leader or a sporting star. If this is you, omit this section from your CV and spend more time detailing your core skills and strengths.

■ **More than four/five achievements**

This is a nice problem to have. To ensure each achievement receives the attention it deserves, split them into different headings, i.e. Awards, Scholarships, Extracurricular Activities and Achievements.

CANDIDATES WITH MORE THAN TWO YEAR'S WORK EXPERIENCE

This section can be entitled 'Career Highlights', 'Key Achievements', 'Selected Achievements' or 'Recent Achievements/Accomplishments'.

When compiling your achievements, reflect on where you have made a difference.

With the last five years in mind, give some thought to:

■ where you saved or made money for the company;
■ initiatives introduced that saved time, money or improved processes;
■ problems solved;
■ awards won;
■ promotions received;
■ commendations by peers, customers/clients or management;
■ examples of where you have exceeded expectations of peers, customers/ clients or management;
■ examples of where you have outperformed your peers;
■ anything else you have been particularly proud of.

To jog your memory, refer to performance appraisals. Your line manager will often identify where you have excelled or exceeded expectations, what your strengths are etc. Similarly, colleagues, current and past, or ex-bosses may provide you with a good insight into your strengths and achievements.

Constructing your achievements section
1. Begin writing down various possibilities.
2. Determine what your personal involvement was in each situation.
3. Write down what the outcome or business benefit was, quantifying if possible.

Example:

> *Original Statement:* Grew Sales.
> *Revised Statement:* Introduced a consultative selling approach which led to a 40% increase in sales within three months.

In summary – Express the task, the action and the result.

Rules
- Include between three and five achievements.
- Ideally, incorporate achievements from the last five years. Only provide achievements from earlier years if they are particularly relevant to the job been applied for.
- List your achievements in reverse chronological order, i.e. most recent first. The alternative is to list the most impressive ones first, but in this instance be sure to omit the dates from each achievement.
- Keep your achievements relevant to your target position and include only commercial achievements. If you have graduated fairly recently it is acceptable to include academic achievements, examples of awards won or examples of where you demonstrated leadership or initiative.
- Keep achievements concise, i.e. no longer than two/three sentences and no longer than four lines in total. Do not provide all the detail – leave the reader wanting more.
- Provide details of what you have achieved, not what others have achieved. Expand on what your involvement in a task has been and the outcome or benefit to the business/clients/team.

- Focus on the results of your actions and quantify wherever possible.
- With respect to functional CVs, focus on including achievements that demonstrate your transferable skills or those that will be particularly relevant to your target position.

Difficulties that you may face

- **It's my job**

  The problem many people experience is they view what they have achieved as part of their everyday job. It is important to differentiate yourself from a candidate doing the same or a similar job, so think about examples of where you have gone the extra mile for a customer, client, manager, colleague or peer. Think about examples of where you have added value or where you have excelled at a certain task.

- **Unable to quantify your achievements**

  In some industries, for example, sales and operations, it is fairly easy to quantify your achievements as you can highlight quite simply how much business you brought on, how much turnover increased by or how much money you saved when you implemented a specific system. It is more difficult in other industries, for example, you may work as a researcher or a secretary. Although your achievements may not be quantifiable, they will still be recognised as achievements nonetheless. Rather than focus on quantifying, focus on detailing the result of your actions.

- **No relevant achievements**

  Incorporate your achievements if they are impressive, otherwise, omit this section and incorporate your achievements under each of your respective positions. In the case of a functional CV, if your achievements demonstrate potential and will provide an employer with an indication of what you are capable of, include two or three.

- **Too many achievements**

  Select four or five of your most impressive achievements; the balance can be incorporated under employment history.

■ Too few achievements

Should you only have one or two achievements, omit this section. Either entitle your 'Key Skills' section, 'Key Skills and Achievements', and combine the two sections, or add the achievement(s) under your employment history.

■ No achievements

Should you have very little experience, truly no achievements to speak of or honestly do not feel that you have achieved anything substantial to date, leave this section out altogether. Focus attention on other areas of strength whether it be training or key skills, employment history or computer literacy.

Points to note

■ If you have worked for many companies, you may include the company name within the point or at the end of the sentence in brackets. This is more impressive if you have worked for a blue-chip company.

■ You can incorporate dates of when each event was achieved, but this is not mandatory.

Examples:

Set up a successful business from scratch, developing, running and managing a team that provides a first-class, reliable service within a highly competitive environment.

Oversaw the construction of an Assessment Centre, a 10-week project that involved managing a team of 12. The successful project was delivered on time and to budget (£200k).

Implemented new operational procedures for the call centre within six weeks of joining the firm, which increased conversions by 15%.

Played a fundamental part in developing and growing the company from five to 65 staff in an 18-month period, and doubling turnover over the same.

Pitched for and won three major contracts for XYZ company worth £2.5m annually.

Projected and managed several major refurbishments projects including a £3.5m project for XYZ Hotel, which consisted of a major extension and additions in the form of a new spa and restaurant.

Initiated and received board approval to significantly change the company's client relation strategies. Transformed direct door-to-door sales policies and increased annual sales by 10%.

Consistently commended for dealing effectively with demanding and difficult customers.

Exposed and corrected a clerical oversight that resulted in an annual saving of £100k.

Seconded to the US for a period of 12 months to set up an international contact centre which involved recruiting, coaching and training a team of seven, and appointing a manager to oversee the operation.

Formulated and introduced a company manual that exceeded all current legislative requirements.

Built and opened a new restaurant, which grew to a profitable concern turning over £1.2m within under a year.

Established formal release management processes and procedures, obtaining buy-in from divisions across the company and the CTO.

Projected managed the successful integration of two trading systems, which were implemented with zero downtime or loss to the business.

Transformed an under-performing teenage magazine from a static readership pool into a vibrant, financially viable and profitable production.

Instigated a project saving plan across several product areas of the group, gaining board approval to implement the company's first ever procurement system solution worth £2m.

Streamlined procedures within the finance department, resulting in an immediate cost saving of £0.5m, and sourced new suppliers securing above average discounts and a further cost saving of £0.25m per year.

Consistently exceeded sales targets and was awarded 'Regional Sales Person of the Year' for three consecutive years.

Delivered a high standard of operation and budgetary control to XYZ County Council, saving the company £10m over three years, four times more than anticipated.

Turned around a previously declining portfolio to an impressive 125% year-on-year revenue growth within just eight months of being appointed.

Designed and developed specialised moulding products within the construction industry, substantially reducing production costs by 15% whilst still maintaining quality.

Progressed from a Trainee to a Manager within just four years of joining XYZ Company.

In 2005, achieved the highest ever-average occupancy rate for a hotel in the Bahamas (92%) and doubled room revenue over the same period.

Implemented various marketing initiatives and distribution programmes, which led to XYZ plc capturing a further 10% market share in its core product area.

Significantly increased customer satisfaction levels through providing consistently high levels of customer service and training junior members of the team to do the same.

Joined XYZ Ltd as a Trainee and was quickly promoted to Assistant Manager just 14 months later.

Performed two simultaneous roles at XYZ company for a six month period following the departure of the Area Manager.

Negotiated discounted rates with suppliers, reducing operating costs by 8% per annum.

Delivered technical services to XYZ plc and introduced new technology that transformed processes and reduced operational expenditure by 12%.

Consistently commended by management for meeting deadlines and for integrating with staff across the business.

Key contributor for the design and implementation of a number of successful projects that significantly reduced maintenance costs and downtime.

Secured new business contracts with several key players in the industry valued at £2.5m per annum.

Successfully managed several tender processes and bids on behalf of XYZ plc, 25% of which were awarded to the company.

Orchestrated the successful turnaround of ABC business unit by revitalising both the product range and sales strategy; delivered 125% revenue growth in two years.

Designed and distributed literature and posters for the marketing and advertising of community services, increasing awareness by 25%.

Introduced new processes and procedures to the finance function; dramatically improved the quality of reporting and reduced the production of management accounts by seven days.

Developed and implemented an Excel spreadsheet that enabled the comparative analysis of all company expenditure.

Played a fundamental role in developing XYZ's position in the European market place, which increased market share by 10% in 12 months.

Set up a newly created department for XYZ plc, which included recruiting and training all staff, and implementing all operational procedures.

With all of the above in mind, spend some time thinking about what you have achieved. Utilise the action words at the end of the book to help you detail each one.

CHAPTER 12

WORK HISTORY

Your CV will now be starting to take shape. Once you have compiled this next section, you will be 95% of the way there.

Work history is an area that will receive a lot of attention from a prospective employer. Unfortunately, too many people get it wrong! This chapter covers how to write effective, interesting content. It includes experts opinions, provides several examples and details how to overcome common problems.

CHRONOLOGICAL AND CHRONO-FUNCTIONAL CVS

This next section is split into candidates with less than and candidates with more than two years' work experience, as what you emphasise will be dependent on how much experience you have.

Candidates with less than two years' work experience

First-time job seekers are often unsure of what and how much to include. Too many of you discount summer jobs or voluntary work if it is unrelated to what you are looking to apply for. It is important to realise that any experience you have gained is very relevant.

> ' *A common thing with university level graduates, they assume that the summer job they had that was essentially to earn pocket money, is not relevant. To us it's very relevant if somebody has had the get-up-and-go to work 20 hours a week to supplement their pocket money, and help them fund their way through college.* '
>
> *Jonathan Jones at Goldman Sachs (Investment Bank)*

> '*Your experience could be in sports where you've organised a competition or a league, and you've managed that. It could be at school where you've organised a trip. I'm looking for the skills that are relevant to the role.*'
>
> Mark Thomas at Tesco (Retailer)

Whether you have worked as a cashier, a dog walker or a sales assistant, you are bound to have gained or honed some very valuable skills. Holding down a summer or a part-time job also tells a prospective employer a lot about you. So include it all – everything from summer jobs and internships through to voluntary work experience, no matter how trivial the role may seem.

Compiling the content

This section can be headed 'Work Experience', 'Work History' or 'Employment History'. If you have had or are currently in a full-time role, you could split your work history into 'Work Experience' and 'Professional Experience'. 'Work Experience' is often considered to be summer or part-time work or could include internships. Any voluntary work should be expressed separately and is covered in a separate chapter.

Begin by writing down all your positions, starting with the most recent and working backwards. Detail the company name, location, start/end dates, and your job title. Leave half a page between each role providing you with space to add a number of bullet points under each role. It is often valuable to provide a short description of the company below the company name, particularly if the company is obscure.

The type of information you can include under each of your roles are:

1. Duties and responsibilities

Denote your main tasks but rather than listing a duty or responsibility, use power words to describe what you actual involvement was and what you achieved.

Example: if you were a waitress, rather than saying '*Serving customers*', you could say:

Provided a consistently high level of service to customers owing to a thorough understanding of the menu, wine list and daily specials.

2. Initiatives introduced

Consider including proposals or ideas you recommended that were later implemented.

Examples:

Developed an Excel spreadsheet that considerably enhanced the accuracy of information.

Designed a rating system that significantly improved the quality of potential leads.

3. Examples of money made or saved for the company

Companies are in business to make money so if you can provide examples at this early stage in your career as to how you may have made or saved money for a company, this will be of great interest to a prospective employer.

Examples:

In conjunction with the Sales Director, secured a deal with a major retailer, worth £100k per annum.

Introduced and implemented a process that improved web conversions by 250%.

4. Targets met and exceeded – company and personal

As with the point above, the ability to meet or exceed company targets demonstrates your ability to make money and shows drive. The ability to meet your own personal targets displays focus and commitment.

Example:

Consistently met and exceeded sales targets and was rewarded with a 'Top Account Opener' award and £500 within first two months of joining.

5. Promotions or offers of full-time employment

Receiving an advancement or being offered a permanent position demonstrates your potential to a prospective employer, particularly if it occurs within a short timescale.

Example:

Promoted to Supervisor of XYZ Company after a period of four months, becoming the youngest supervisor within the XYZ Franchise.

6. Emphasise team working and/or leadership capabilities

Provide details of any projects you may have worked on or managed. Include examples of where you may have been involved in training or supporting staff, and anything else that will demonstrate your ability to lead or work as part of a team.

Examples:

Worked as part of a team to plan, design and deliver an intranet for a PR company.

Managed a small team of four Administrators across two branches and provided product training to all new starters.

7. Honing or learning new skills

Specify any skills and knowledge gained or learned particularly if those skills will be relevant to your target position. These can include anything from honing problem solving skills and resolving customer queries through to leadership and communication skills.

Examples:

Gained an excellent knowledge of the principles of book-keeping and accountancy.

Developed event management skills from assisting with the co-ordination of various high profile events.

8. Awards

Have you received any awards in recognition for a job well done or good grades at university, school or college?

Example:

Awarded a certificate of recognition from the Head of Department for services in the community, in a Student Ambassador role.

9. Commendations

Have you received praise, written or verbal, from a colleague, manager, peer or client? Including one or two recommendations can validate your worth to a company.

Example:

Commended by the Team Leader for providing consistently high levels of customer service and for remaining calm in heated situations.

Include anything else that you have been particularly proud of. In each case, express what your personal involvement was and the outcome or result. Furnish tangible examples and quantify wherever possible.

Rules

- Ensure it is obvious whether work was part-time, full-time or voluntary. This can be achieved by heading each one separately or merely including the job type directly after your job title in brackets. Voluntary work is best kept separate.

- Aim to provide three or four points under each role. Your most recent roles should be more detailed than ones further back.
- Avoid using the word 'responsible' and do your very best to utilise action words to begin each sentence (see list at end of book).
- Where you have had more than one position with the same company, list each one separately.
- If you have too many points, include those statements that are most impressive and do not encourage the reader to say 'so what'.
- Avoid stating the obvious and listing a job description.
- Write in the past tense unless writing about your current role.
- Do not include anything negative.
- Include what you have done, not things that you still hope to do.
- Avoid repetition. If you have done similar tasks in all or some of your previous positions, consider a functional CV or grouping them together.
- Place your most impressive statements first.

Potential problems

1. Obscure job title

Should you have held obscure or company specific job titles, generalise the title so you appeal to the widest possible audience.

2. Many positions held

It is important to include all your work experience but if you have held more than four/five roles, only include detail on those roles:

- most appropriate to your target position; or
- where you made an impact; or
- where you gained/honed key skills that will be relevant to a prospective employer.

The remainder of your positions can be summarised with merely the company name, job title and start/end dates.

3. No work experience

Should you have no work experience, voluntary or otherwise, emphasise other areas in your CV, for example, key skills gained during your studies. Also provide information on any other activities that you may or have been involved in whether it be sporting interests or hobbies.

Examples of work experience

Below are some examples of what content to include under work history and some different ways in which the information can be presented. For more examples refer to the appended CD.

Example 1:

ABC Pub Ltd, London   **Jan 2003–Sept 2004**

Bartender (Part-time)
- *Developed customer facing skills and the ability to remain calm and professional within a fast-paced working environment*
- *Co-ordinated and hosted private and public functions for up to 50 people, honing organisational and planning skills*
- *Assisted with training new staff members*
- *Monitored and maintained stock levels*

Example 2:

Summer 2006   **Cashier, XYZ Limited, Hampshire**
- *Performed general cashier duties for VIP customers, honing customer service and cash handling capabilities*
- *Consistently cross-sold company products and services to new and existing clients; received an 'employee of the month' award for two consecutive months for highest product sales*

Example 3:

Sept 2006–Dec 2006   *ABC plc*

Assistant Event Manager
- *Provided full secretarial and administrative support to a team of three Event Managers*
- *Organised a variety of high-profile events and functions including themed evenings and fund raising events for up to 200 people, all of which were highly successful and achieved high attendance rates*
- *Gained time management skills and honed the ability to work well under pressure*

Example 4:

May 2007 to Date: Administrator, XTC Limited, London
- *Created and maintained an access database that considerably increased productivity*
- *Re-organised the company filing system, significantly reducing the amount of time required to locate and access client files*
- *Successfully cleared all outstanding filing and a backlog of data entry tasks during this period*
- *Honed organisational, planning and team working skills*

May 2006 to Sept 2006: PA, RLC Limited, London
- *Managed the daily schedule for the Sales Director and dealt with all incoming and outgoing mail*
- *Maintained daily contact with foreign clients, updating them of any contract changes*
- *Gained valuable communication skills and the ability to effectively manage a heavy workload under pressure*

Example 5:

ABC plc, London   **Jan 2003 – Sept 2004**

Medical Technologist (Internship)
- *Received detailed training within Microbiology and Cytology departments*
- *Investigated and analysed clinical specimens, reporting results to the relevant medical staff*

Example 6:

May 2007 to Date: Law Clerk, DGH Limited, London
- *Provided administrative support to lawyers through conducting research and drafting court documents*
- *Booked various appointments for associates and senior partners*
- *Proof read legal documents for various senior partners*
- *Participated in two mock trials, developing communication skills and confidence*

Sept 2005 to Dec 2006: Sales Agent, SRC plc, Surrey
- *Initiated business launches for potential customers to demonstrate product range*
- *Devised a new sales pitch and approach, which was later adopted by the entire team*
- *Consistently converted new enquiries into sales; received several financial rewards in recognition*
- *Gained persuasion and negotiation skills*

With the above in mind, spend some time writing down as many points that you can think of under each role. It is easier to eliminate statements than to add ones.

Candidates with more than two years' work experience

A common pitfall is that people tend to produce a job description rather than focusing on what they have achieved or what skills or knowledge they have gained or honed. We all know that it is an accountant's job to produce a set of year-end accounts or that it is a sales professional's role to bring on new business. Do not risk patronising or alienating the reader by stating the obvious. Instead, explain what you have delivered in relation to your duties and responsibilities, providing tangible examples and quantifying wherever possible.

> ‘ *The biggest thing that I look for in a CV is legacy; so, what value has an individual added to their particular organisation during the time in which they've done a particular role? So, what I'm particularly looking at is contribution to bottom line profitability, sales, what are the metrics, what are the key performance indicators that that person has been responsible for and what have they personally delivered.*
>
> *Later on he goes on to say: 'My key principle is that past performance predicts future performance, so the essence of a CV for me is again about key achievements.* ’
>
> *Tesco (Retailer – Mark Thomas)*

> ‘ *What we're really looking for is evidence of what somebody's done in their lives, not evidence of what they think they are.* ’
>
> *Odgers, Ray and Berndtson (Executive Search Firm – Will Dawkins)*

As a way of reflecting how your accomplishments will sell your ability to an employer, a CV should have a good combination of features and benefits. Adrian Cojocaru uses the analogy of someone looking to purchase a car.

> ‘ *If you go and buy a car, you know that the features of the car are: alloy wheels, a big stereo and a big engine. The benefits are: low fuel consumption, low CO2 emissions, it was voted the best car for three consecutive years and families with kids prefer it. So again, you want to know the features of the person but you also want to know the benefits. The benefits would need to be very precise and descriptive, detailing what a person has achieved.* ’
>
> *Mars Drinks (FMCG – Adrian Cojocaru)*

Compiling the content

This section can be headed 'Work History', 'Professional Experience', 'Employment History' or 'Career History'.

Note down all of your roles since leaving school, college or university starting with the most recent and working backwards. Detail the company name, location, start/end dates and your job title. Leave half a page between each role providing you with space to add a number of bullet points under each role. It is often valuable to provide a short description of the company below the company name, particularly if the company is obscure.

Under each role begin writing down the following:

1. Duties and responsibilities

Denote your main tasks but rather than listing a duty or responsibility, use power words to describe what your actual involvement was and what you achieved.

Example: if you were an Administrator rather than saying *'Filing and answering the phone and email'*, you could say:

Maintain and develop the department's filing system for four senior managers. In 2007, automated the entire system allowing managers to access client files within seconds.

Provide support to customers, handling queries received via email and on the phone.

2. Initiatives introduced

Consider any proposals or ideas you may have suggested that were later implemented. This can be as simple as developing an Excel spreadsheet to improve the accuracy of information, through to implementing a new process or system that reduced operational costs by 20% per annum.

Example:

> *Redesigned the layout of the facility, which reduced double handling of equipment and increased the quality of the end product.*

3. Examples of where you made or saved money

Companies are in business to make money so it is important, where possible, to provide examples of where you have made or saved money for a company. In some industries this is easier than others. You can also provide examples of where you may have saved time or resource.

Examples:

> *Received approval to outsource the company's payroll, improving reliability of payroll and saving the company £40K per year.*
>
> *Instrumental in securing two new clients for XYZ Company, which saw company revenue increase by 30%.*

4. Targets met and exceeded, company and personal

As with the point above, the ability to meet or exceed targets demonstrates your ability to make money and shows gravitas. The ability to meet your own personal targets displays focus and commitment.

Example:

> *Consistently exceeded quarterly sales targets of £50k, achieving 20% higher than any other colleague.*

5. Promotions

Recall examples of where you may have deputised for a manager, or were headhunted/approached to work for a company.

Examples:

Progressed from Sales Executive to Managing Director of ABC Limited over a period of eight years.

Promoted to Regional Manager within two years of joining; now responsible for managing a team of 80 staff and five units worth £15m per annum.

6. Emphasise team working and/or leadership capabilities

Provide details of any projects you may have worked on or managed. Include examples of where you may have been involved in training or supporting staff, and anything that will demonstrate your ability to lead or work as part of a team.

Examples:

Manage one of the toughest technology departments in the derivatives department of ABC plc, which consists of 50 staff based both in London and New York, and 1,200 support staff.

Acted as a mentor to a number of up and coming managers, providing them with comprehensive training on effectively running a unit

7. Honing or learning new skills

Specify any special skills or knowledge that you possess, that have enabled you to perform a task well.

Example:

Gained a thorough understanding of various HR issues including disciplinary procedures.

8. Awards you might have won

Have you received any awards in recognition for a job well done?

Example:

Nominated for St. Mary's 'Distinguished Teacher's Award' in 2007

9. Commendations or endorsements

Have you received praise, written or verbal, from a colleague, manager, peer or client? Including one or two recommendations can validate your worth to a company. Do not provide more than two or three throughout your CV and do not include testimonials.

Example:

Commended by line manager for consistently exceeding company targets.

10. Problems solved

Employers are interested in how you can solve their problems, so provide demonstrable examples of how and what problems you have solved for other organisations.

Example:

Transformed the business from a loss-making concern of £7m in 2006 to a profitable enterprise with annual turnover of £6m per annum in 2008.

11. Other accomplishments

Include anything else you have been particularly proud of, from how you have performed in relation to your peers, to where you have made a positive contribution. Consider examples of where you have gone the extra mile for the business, clients or colleagues.

In each instance, provide detail of your personal involvement and the outcome/ result. Furnish tangible examples and quantify wherever possible.

Non-managerial staff

For non-managerial staff, it may be appropriate to include where you fit into the reporting structure and any significant responsibilities you have had, for example, training new members of the team, mentoring staff, assisting on certain projects, making recommendations etc.

Managerial staff

If you manage a budget or have full P&L responsibility, it may be pertinent to emphasise the size of your budget as this gives the prospective employer an understanding of the level of responsibility you are accustomed to.

If you manage or have managed a team, provide details of how many staff you manage and how your team breaks down. Include whether you are involved in training, coaching, motivating, KPIs, target setting etc. If you have not included it under the key skills section, provide the reader with an understanding of your management style.

Some pointers

- Be detailed about your most recent role and less so thereafter. For chronological CVs, it is suggested that you have between five and seven points for your current role and one less for each role thereafter, with a minimum of two points per role. With chrono-functional CVs, as you will have quite an in-depth 'Key Skills' section, it is recommended that you have between four and five points for your current role and maybe two/three for earlier positions.
- It is not necessary to provide detailed information about roles held more than 10 years ago. These roles can merely be listed under a heading of 'Early Career' or 'Pre 19XX'.
- Do not include any summer jobs, part-time jobs, temporary work or internships unless particularly relevant to your target position.
- Generally, provide detail of your last three or four roles, any more and space will become an issue. If you have held numerous positions, consider grouping similar ones together or summarising them under a separate section entitled 'Early Career'. Simply list the company name, job title and start/leaving dates.
- Avoid using the word 'responsible' and do your very best to utilise the action words at the end of the book to begin each sentence.

- Do not produce a job description. Select the most salient points of what you do on a day-to-day basis and those that are most interesting, and expand on them.
- Write in the past tense unless you are writing about your current role.
- Do not include anything negative.
- Include what you have done not things that you hope to still do.
- Do not become repetitive; if you have done similar tasks in all or some of your previous positions, a functional CV may be the solution.
- Do not include achievements already mentioned in your key achievements section. Repetition reduces the impact of your CV.
- Place your most impressive statements first.
- If you have too many points, include those statements that are most impressive and do not encourage the reader to say 'so what'.

Potential problems

1. Employment dates
- If you have had short employment gaps, i.e. a few months here and there, do not include the month that you started and left the company but just the year, for example 1995–1999 as opposed to Mar 1995–Apr 1999.
- Should there be obvious gaps in your employment history consider producing a functional CV.

2. Career breaks
- If you have taken time out to have children, taken a sabbatical or travelled in the last 10 years, mention this on your CV rather than leave a glaring gap. The last 10 years of your career needs to be accounted for to avoid red flags being raised.

Leila Bliss at KPMG had this to say:
If they've been looking for a job or if they've been unemployed, it's better to know that than not know.

3. Job titles
- Keep job titles generic as you need to appeal to as many people as possible.

- To avoid pigeon-holing oneself, be specifically vague, for example, instead of junior accountant Level II, just use accountant.

4. Contractor

- If you have been a contractor and have worked on several short assignments, an option would be to replace your 'Employment History' section with a section entitled 'Recent Projects' or 'Selected Projects'. Here you can list five or six projects and provide details of your involvement in each one and the outcome or business benefit.
- Make it clear that you have been contracting to avoid appearing as a 'job hopper'. Refer to yourself as a 'Contractor', adding the word 'contract' next to your job title or heading your employment history as 'Contracts'.
- If you have held several short contracting assignments that have been similar in nature, use the name of the agency as the Company Name and the Company Name within the content.

Example:

Michael Page: London   *2006–Date*

Contractor – Investment Banking
- *Developed numerous spreadsheets for the credit department of XYZ plc which, combined, saved around 30 man-hours per week.*
- *Identified a shortcoming in one of ABC Ltd's systems used to detect customers in unauthorised overdraft; if left undetected this would have cost the company several million pounds.*

5. **You have only worked for one company**
- Provide details of all jobs held with the company to show progression. Keep the most recent three or four roles separate, any roles thereafter can be summarised or combined if similar. If tasks performed in each role are similar or the same, consider a functional CV otherwise you will have a very repetitive CV that will create no impact.

Example:

XYZ BANK: London	***1980–Date***
Director of Customer Relations	*2004–Date*
■ Provide around five to six points	
Regional Director	*2002–2004*
■ Provide around four to five points	
Manager, Business Centre	*1999–2002*
■ Provide around three to four points	
Manager, Customer Relationships	*1997–1999*
■ Provide around three points	
Various Assistant Manager and Clerical Positions	*1980–1997*

8. Obscure company

If you have worked abroad or for a relatively unknown organisation in the UK, provide a short description of the company. This provides the reader with an understanding of the type and size of organisations you have experience of working for.

For candidates applying from abroad, one of our experts had this to say:

'*We are less likely to know the institution they're coming from so they should provide some further information about the type and size of the organisation. I'm not talking about reams but a point or two would be helpful.*'

Leila Bliss at KPMG

9. Providing confidential Information

■ You may be concerned about providing certain details like the company name. It is perfectly acceptable to state 'a National Chain' or 'Investment Bank'. The company name can be provided at interview.

- It is often beneficial to incorporate the name of blue-chip companies on your CV as they attract attention. If, however, you are uncomfortable about providing names of clients, the size of an account or company turnover, then leave it out. Some companies are precious about this information and may have requested that you sign a confidentiality agreement when you joined.

It must be noted, however, that potential employers or agencies are obliged to treat CVs in the strictest of confidence.

Examples of work history

Below are examples of what can be included in your work history and how to present the information. As with the examples below, the focus should be on what you achieved, and the outcome/result. Where possible, quantify each point.

Example 1:

Feb 2007–Present　　　*XYZ Insurance Agency, Hertfordshire*
Director and Founder

- *Set up this successful business from scratch; the business now employs 25 staff and turned over £400k in its first year of trading.*
- *Manage the day-to-day operations including all administration, internal business processes, workflow, policy making and strategy.*
- *Regularly negotiate with suppliers thereby securing preferential rates and terms.*
- *Secured three major corporate accounts in first six months, winning business previously held by major players in the industry.*

Example 2:

XYZ Company, Surrey   **2005–Date**
Manufacturers of road construction and maintenance plant and equipment

Administration Officer/PA
- *Provide full secretarial and administrative support to a team of five senior managers.*
- *Devise and implement standard processes and procedures on behalf of the administration team, in compliance with company policy.*
- *Organise conferences, exhibitions and other large corporate events throughout the year, for up to 500 representatives.*
- *Created and maintain an access database to effectively co-ordinate supplier contracts, which has significantly improved the servicing and renewal processes.*
- *Assisted the business unit with clearing a backlog of invoices.*

Example 3:

XYZ IT Company, London   **Feb 2006–Date**

Technical Manager
Appointed to deliver major internet systems to clients across Hertfordshire:
- *Managed several technical teams ranging from two to 20 developers.*
- *Forged important relationships with new and existing clients in order to understand their exacting requirements.*
- *Played a fundamental role in shaping the strategic direction of the department and ensured each technical team adopted best practices and process to facilitate the smooth technical delivery of each client project.*
- *Provided detailed plans, developed appropriate documentation and produced regular project status reports for each project.*
- *Successfully delivered completed, working and tested projects within agreed timescales and on budget.*

Example 4:

May 2007 to date: Contracts Manager, ABC Construction, Nottingham

- *Supervise a team of 30 operatives and up to 10 subcontractors.*
- *Initiated and implemented preventative maintenance, improving client relations and significantly reducing the likelihood of customer complaints.*
- *Seconded to XYZ Ltd for a period of six months to turnaround this under-performing concern. Implemented operational procedures and restructured departments, which saw each business unit meeting targets and achieving margins for the first time in 18 months.*
- *Maintain accurate up-to-date records including site diaries, health and safety records, and ledgers covering personnel, payroll, supplies and inventory.*
- *Compile and submit quarterly P&L reports to senior management.*

Example 5:

If you have held more than one position with the same company express as follows:

XYZ Company, London   Aug 2006–Jul 2008

Sales Manager   Mar 2006–Jul 2009
- *Managed, trained, motivated and developed a team of six field representatives, all of whom frequently exceeded sales targets.*
- *Monitored market trends and competitor activity, identifying possible new business areas worth a potential £1m per annum.*
- *Introduced a new product, diversifying business activities and increasing company revenue by 10% in the first six months of its introduction.*
- *Maintained positive customer relationships through adopting a consultative sales approach; achieved a 20% increase in revenue in first eight months.*

Field Representative   *Aug 2005–Feb 2006*

- *Sold an extensive range of corporate FMCG merchandise to SME clients across the UK. Increased the number of new enquiries to the business by 20% and secured over 50 new accounts.*
- *Provided support and guidance to less experienced sales staff.*
- *Developed a customer database to analyse buying patterns and individual customer requirements, in order to deliver a tailor-made service.*
- *Consistently achieved targets and business objectives, and was promoted to Sales Manager six months after joining.*

Tip

Should the company be unknown, it is important to provide a company description which should be expressed below the company name. Keep it brief, one sentence, and if relevant provide details of the company size (number of employees and/or turnover). If you provide a company description for one company, keep this consistent throughout your CV, providing descriptions for all the companies you have worked for. Should you have worked for just one unknown company incorporate the company description into the body of the text, for example, 'oversaw operations of this multi-million pound retail business, which included a warehouse, distribution centre and call centre'.

Once you have read this section and digested it, spend some time detailing your 'Work History', utilising the action words at the end of this book. Write down as many points that you can think of under each role. It is easier to eliminate statements than to add ones later on.

As mentioned repeatedly, you do not want to produce a job description. Once you have completed this section, review each point under each role. Where possible, let the points raise questions as this creates curiosity and improves your chances of being invited to interview. Should a statement be 'so what', it needs to be expanded upon to make it impressive and interesting, otherwise it should be eliminated. Some examples will now follow.

Examples:

Original statement

- Responsible for the entire accounts function and measurement of Key Performance Indicators.

Revised statement

- *Lead, managed and motivated the entire finance function consisting of five senior accountants and three assistants.*
- *Developed and implemented a set of KPIs that are now standard across the group.*

Original statement

- Set up both computerised and manual systems to ensure the efficient gathering, sorting and storing of information.

Revised statement

- *Created and implemented several computerised and manual systems, significantly improving the efficiency of gathering, sorting and storing of information.*

Original statement

- Turned around an under-performing division and team.

Revised statement

- *Restructured, built and grew a previously disparate function consisting of a low-skilled, unmotivated team, into a driven, focused team that delivered the best results in company history.*

FUNCTIONAL CVS

This section should be entitled 'Career Summary'. The intention of producing a functional CV is to detract from your career history. Irrespective of how much experience you have, all that is required is a summary of your work history.

Compiling the content

Write down all the positions you have held starting with the most recent. Detail the company name, location, start and end dates for each one.

Some pointers

- Ensure there are no gaps in your career summary and each year is accounted for. This can be achieved in the following ways:
  - group similar jobs;
  - if you have had several temporary positions or contracts, you can group as 'Various Temporary Assignments' or 'Various Contracts';
  - avoid using months on your CV, just the year you commenced and left;
  - mention things like travel, career breaks or secondments.
- Keep job titles generic as you need to appeal to as many people as possible.
- It is only necessary to go back 10 years.
- List your roles in reverse chronological order, i.e. most recent first.

EXAMPLES

Example 1:

2004–Date	**Career Break: Part-time studies and Travel**
2002–2004	**XYZ Company, London**
2003–2004	*Regional Sales Manager*
2002–2003	*Area Manager*
2001–2002	**ABC Limited, Edinburgh**
	Assistant Account Manager
2000–2001	**DCT plc, London**
	Client's Assistant
1998–2000	**Various Contracts** (Deutche Bank, Coutts, JP Morgan)

Example 2:

ABC Ltd, London *Customer Service Officer*	**2007–Date**
Career Break: Full-time Mother	**2006–2007**
DGH plc, London *Marketing Consultant*	**2003–2005**
PQR Ltd, London *Claims Advisor*	**2000–2002**
XYX Ltd, London *Office Accounts Junior*	**1998–1999**

Example 3:

2006 to Date	**General Sales Manager: IXY Drinks Company,** Surrey
2004 to 2006	**Export Sales Manager: MXY plc,** London
2002 to 2004	**Area Sales Manager/Sales Associate: Various**
1999 to 2002	**Telesales: DEG Limited,** Hertfordshire
Pre-1998	**Early career in Accountancy**

Example 4:

2007–Date	**Social Host, ABC Limited:** London
2005–2007	**Croupier, CDA Limited:** Portsmouth
2001–2004	**Waitress/Bartender, XYZ Ships:** Portsmouth
1998–2001	**Personal Assistant, XYZ plc:** London

Take the time to now put together your career summary. For more examples, refer to the appended CD.

CHAPTER 13

VOLUNTARY WORK

Offering your services as a volunteer not only assists your community and allows you to help others, but it can enrich your life and work experience. Voluntary work or unpaid work experience can also bolster your CV as it shows a prospective employer both commitment and a willingness to learn. This is even more so if you have gained experience that is directly relevant to your target position.

WHEN TO INCLUDE VOLUNTARY WORK ON YOUR CV

For those with less than two years' work experience, it is important to divulge all employment, voluntary or otherwise. Entry-level job seekers who have participated as a volunteer are likely to have gained confidence and self-awareness amongst other skills, and this will be of interest to a prospective employer.

For those with more than two years' experience, include voluntary work only if it will be supportive to your application and/or relevant to your target position. Some of you may view it as massaging your ego and you may be reluctant to include it, but a prospective employer likes to see a willingness to help others and a commitment to your community. Voluntary work can tell a prospective employer a lot about you as an individual; it may very well add credibility to your application, and it is more often than not seen in a very positive light.

6 60% of HR respondents stated that the details of voluntary activities are a useful addition to a CV. 9

CMC Survey 2007

This section should immediately follow your employment history and need not be very detailed. Describe your activities and what you have achieved. Dates and company names need not be included.

EXAMPLES

Example 1:

- *A qualified Mountain Leader who regularly organises various outdoor pursuits for groups of children.*

Example 2:

May 1998–Aug 1998   *XYZ School, Class Room Assistant*

- *Provided support to the Head of English, supervising the class in her absence and assisting children suffering with reading and learning difficulties.*
- *Assisted with preparing classes and planning activity sessions.*

Example 3:

- *Co-ordinate and plan several fund raising initiatives each year for XYZ Charity. To date, have raised in excess of £500k.*

Example 4:

Volunteer   *2005–2007*
- *Organised two fund raising events which, combined, raised £5,000. Utilised the funds to set up a crèche, which benefited 10 families and 22 children.*
- *Designed and created a company website for a not-for-profit organisation; developed all the content, organised hosting and identified potential partners.*

Take some time now to detail your experience, if relevant to your circumstances.

CHAPTER 14

PROFESSIONAL ASSOCIATIONS/ MEMBERSHIPS

The next step is to list any professional memberships, affiliations or memberships. As per Wikipedia, a professional association or professional society is: *'an organisation, usually non-profit that exists to further a particular profession, to protect both the public interest and the interests of professionals'*.

Professional bodies are often involved in developing and monitoring professional educational programs, updating skills, and perform professional certification to denote that a person possesses qualifications in the subject area. Membership of a professional body is sometimes synonymous with certification. In some professions, membership of a professional body can form the primary formal basis for gaining entry to and setting up practice within the profession.

Not everyone will be a member of or belong to a professional, regulatory or student body, but if you do, this is where you will include the details. Listing your membership shows dedication to your career, if relevant to your chosen vocation. Only include memberships that are relevant to your target position. If, however, you are in a profession like PR, marketing, sales, property or management, include all of them as it shows wide networks.

Do not include religious or political associations; a CV is a representation of your professional, not your personal life.

If you are not part of any professional associations or affiliations, this section should be omitted from your CV.

HOW TO PRESENT THE INFORMATION
This section can be entitled 'Professional Affiliations', 'Professional Associations' or 'Memberships'. Include the name of the organisation, acronym (if appropriate), followed by the date you became a member.

Examples:

Member of the British Institute of Innkeeping (MBII)   2005–Date

Associate Chartered Institute of Bankers (ACIB) since 1984

Member of the Institute of Operations Management (IOM) since 1997

Associate member of the Institute of Management   2002
Consultants

Member of the British Computer Society   2000

Fellow of the Institute of Sales and Marketing   2003
Management (UK)

Professional member of the Chartered Institute of Personnel &
Development (CIPD), 2007

CHAPTER 15

PUBLICATIONS AND PATENTS

This section will not be relevant to everyone. Publications and/or patents only need to be included if relevant to your target position.

LISTING PUBLICATIONS

When listing publications, the following should be noted:

1. Have separate headings for:
    (a) Publications – with sub-heading Articles, Book Contributions and Reviews (if appropriate);
    (b) Research Papers;
    (c) Courses and Conferences Attended;
    (d) Teaching Experience.
2. List in reverse chronological order, i.e. most recent first.
3. Indicate authors according to original order and indicate the first and last page of the article.
4. Detail the full name of the article or paper, and the date it was published.

If you are an academic, it is advisable to include an Appendix detailing your publications and papers. Otherwise, include those that are most relevant and state that 'more information on publications is available on request'.

LISTING PATENTS

When listing a patent, specify whether the patent has been granted or is pending, the patent number, and the country in which it was awarded.

CHAPTER 16

COMPUTER/TECHNICAL SKILLS

Computers are an essential part of the commercial environment, so regardless of your background or specialisation, whether you come from a technical background or whether you are a pilot, teacher or surgeon, it is imperative that you are computer literate.

If you are a new entrant to the job market, the chances are quite high that you would have been exposed to computers at school, college or university.

The benefits of being computer literate are increased employability and greater earning potential and as such, whether you have completed a course or are self-taught, is it important to detail your proficiency with various packages, systems or programming languages.

Non-technical and technical backgrounds are now discussed separately.

NON-TECHNICAL BACKGROUNDS

Under a title of 'Computer Skills', 'Technical Skills' or 'IT Skills', indicate your computer literacy by describing your ability with each package or system.

EXAMPLES

Example 1:

- *Fully conversant with Microsoft Word and Excel; the Internet.*
- *Experience of working on various operating systems including Windows XP, MAC and Dos.*
- *Familiar with the mechanics of web design.*

Example 2:

- *Proficient user of Microsoft Office – Word, Excel, Access, PowerPoint and Outlook.*
- *Basic understanding of databases including SQL server, My SQL and ORACLE.*
- *Completed introduction using Visual Basic 6.*

Example 3:

- *Highly competent user of Microsoft Word, Excel, Access, Publisher, email and the internet.*
- *Proficient in various programming languages including Microsoft Visual Fox Pro6 and J2EE, and web technologies including Java Script and Dreamweaver MX.*

Should you be responding to a specific position where you are expressly required to have experience with a certain package or system, you need to ensure you draw attention to your computer skills. As such, the information can be expressed in one of four places:

1. in the key skills section on page one of your CV;
2. in your profile statement;
3. move this section to page one of your CV;
4. leave this section on page two, but draw attention to your computer literacy in your covering letter.

TECHNICAL BACKGROUNDS

This section is for those with a technical background or those seeking a role in IT. Under the title of 'Technical Skills', 'IT Skills', or 'Technical Competencies', provide a detailed breakdown of your technical competencies.

How to present the information

The amount of detail provided, and the way the information is expressed, will be dependent on your experience and on what technical skills you are looking to highlight. This section can be presented in one of three ways:

Example 1:

- *Border Gateway Protocol (BGP)/Multi-protocol BGP (MP-BGP).*
- *TCP/Ipv4: OSPF, IS-IS, EIGRP and all other IGPs. TCP/Ipv6: all current protocols.*
- *WAN/LAN: DSL, ATM, FR, ISDN, VPN, VOIP, GSR/XR, C6500, C3750/3550,CSS11500, ASA/PIX.*
- *Cisco Wireless networks 4404 Controllers, 1xxx series Aps and all Cisco Wireless Management software.*
- *MCSE NT4.0, MCSD, A+, Windows (Vista, XP and 2003), Office 2003, Linux and Unix (freeware versions).*
- *Vmware, Checkpoint, HP-Openview, CiscoWorks, Spectrum, Remedy, Smarts, Rancid, Vital Suite, MRTG/Perl and Websense.*

Example 2:

Desktop Operating Systems	*MS-DOS v3.x – v6.x, Windows 3.x – XP, Linux (SuSe, Ubuntu OpenLinux)*
Network Operating Systems	*Windows Server v4.0 – 2003, Novell Netware v3.x – v5.x, Vmware (Workstation/GSX Server)*
Messaging	*Lotus Notes/Domino 4.x/5.x/6.x Server, Exchange 5.5 – 2003, Outlook 97 – XP. Blackberry Server v3.x/4.x*
LAN/WAN Technology	*Switches (Cisco, 3Com, HP), Routers (Cisco 2600, 2500, 1700, 1600)* *Protocols – IPX/SPX, TCP/IP (DNS, DHCP)* *Cabling – 1000BaseT, 100BaseT, 10BaseT, Fibre* *PIX Firewall (520,515)*
Software Packages	*Microsoft Office, Lotus SmartSuite, Adobe, Macromedia, Corel desktop applications*
	Various Anti-Virus solutions – Dr Solomon's, McAfee *Disk Imaging/cloning – Ghost 4/5, Drivecopy* *Helpdesk Software: Quetzal/Utopia/Infoman/Netman* *Backup Software: Arcserve, Brightsor, Tapeware* *Remote Control Software: PcAnywhere, CarbonCopy, NetOp, VNC, Remote Desktop*
Scripting Languages	*Vbscript, HTML, Pascal, Qbasic*

Example 3:

If space is an issue, your technical skills can be expressed as follows:

- *Project* • *Siebel Sytems* • *Oracle OSO* • *Dos*
- *Clarify Clear Sales* • *Visio* • *Windows 3.1*
- *Windows 95/97/98/00/07* • *Frame relay/IP WAN technology*

Where to present the information

If you are seeking a managerial role, this section can be placed after employment history.

If you are seeking a more technical role where your technical skills will be of great interest to a prospective employer, this section should come directly after 'Key Skills' or if not applicable, directly after your 'Profile' on page one of your CV.

Before proceeding to the next chapter, take a few moments to detail your computer literacy.

CHAPTER 17

LANGUAGES

With many companies having global operations, organisations are often looking for candidates with multi-cultural experience and foreign language skills. As such, it is important to provide details of your proficiency with a language whether it be basic, conversational or fluent but only if relevant to the job you are applying for.

> ❝ 81% of HR respondents said that they would like to see language skills included on a CV – especially if language skills are an integral part of the role. ❞
>
> CMC Survey 2007

COMPILING THIS SECTION

Under the title of 'Languages', indicate your level of fluency in each language. Below are some terms that can be used to express your competency:

- Basic knowledge of . . .
- Fluent in . . .
- Conversational . . .
- Read, write and understand . . .
- Native English speaker fluent in . . . with basic . . . language skills
- Good understanding of . . .
- Advanced Spanish and basic French language skills
- Fluent in German (mother-tongue) and English
- Multilingual: fluent in English, Spanish, Russian and French
- Bilingual: French and English

Where to place the information

Should you be applying for a role where you are required to be fluent in a particular language, incorporate your language skills on the first page of your CV either under 'Key Skills' section or in your 'Profile'. Otherwise, this section should appear after 'computer skills'.

Tip

- If you are British and applying to a UK company, do not include that you are fluent in English.
- If English is not your first language, be truthful about your fluency. The same applies to other languages that you include in your CV.
- Should you have no foreign languages that will be applicable to your target position, this section should be excluded.

CHAPTER 18

ADDITIONAL INFORMATION

This section is used to express any other information that may be of interest to a potential employer including driving status, willingness to travel, interests and hobbies, any roles in the military, obligations on a personal level, honours, awards, nominations, charity work, non-executive directorships or anything else that will add value to your application. Again, this section needs to be relevant.

Prior to 2006, many people included personal information such as marital status, nationality and number of dependents on their CV; including your age was compulsory. Today, it is not mandatory to provide personal information about yourself due to Government legislation forbidding employment discrimination. Following the Age Discrimination Act 2006, it became unlawful for employers to discriminate on the basis of age. Consequently it is recommended that your age be omitted from your CV. Additionally, providing information on marital status, race, religion, height, weight, the number of dependents you have and your nationality, provides no bearing on your ability to do the job, and as such, should be excluded from your CV.

INFORMATION THAT CAN BE INCLUDED

1. Driver's licence
Include your driving status if the job you are applying for states that you should hold a specific type of driving licence or if your job is likely to involve travel. Provide details of what licence you hold and in the case of car licence, whether your licence is 'full and clean'. If not clean, i.e. you have points on your licence, state 'full'.

Examples of specialist driving licences:
- Class C and C&E LGV Truck Driving Licence.
- Motorcycle and HGV C+E.

- C1 Licence.
- LGV1 entitlement.

2. Location

Should you be 'willing to relocate or travel', express this here.

> 6 *81% of HR respondents felt that a CV should express a willingness to relocate.* 9
>
> *CMC Survey 2007*

3. Security clearance

If your career requires an active or current security clearance, include this here or make mention of it in your 'Profile Statement'.

Examples of Security Clearance Requirements:

- Secret (S).
- Sensitive Compartmentalised Information (TS/SCI I).
- NSA or CIA.
- Top Secret (TS).
- Cleared to work on Restricted and Confidential Government Systems.
- Achieved high security clearance.

4. Interests and hobbies

It is open to interpretation as to whether this section should be included. The consensus from most of the experts interviewed was:

- If you do include hobbies and/or interests, keep them as relevant as possible.
- Do not incorporate something you did just once.
- Keep it to no more than one or two sentences; do not go on for half a page.
- Avoid including social activities that people are likely to make a judgement on, such as shooting or religion.
- Do not include the stereotypical interests such as 'walking, reading and swimming'.

A prospective employer can tell a lot about a person from their interests and/or hobbies, and having them on a CV can serve as an icebreaker and break down barriers at interview.

> ❛ *It adds colour to the CV.* ❜
>
> *Daniell Morrisey at the BBC*

> ❛ *It helps me visualise what sort of person they are. I think interests and hobbies are actually quite important as it shows people have a balance in life; some people don't have any interests and hobbies and again, that says something about the individual.* ❜
>
> *Giles Crewdson at Korn Ferry*

> ❛ *You've got to be careful about the ones that you put down. Particularly good ones that are relevant in business are activities in the social world, in not-for-profit.* ❜
>
> *Will Dawkins at Odgers, Ray and Berndtson*

You need to make a judgment on whether or not to include your interests and hobbies. Jonathan Jones at Goldman Sachs encapsulates this well:

> ❛ *A candidate's hobbies and interests do not usually have any direct bearing on competencies that are related to the job they're applying for and therefore I would never say that's something that candidates must put on a CV.* ❜
>
> *Jonathan Jones at Goldman Sachs*

It is recommended that you include this section only if by including your interests and hobbies, you are likely to increase your chances of being invited to interview or getting the job because they are directly related to what you do, or because they demonstrate certain skills such as organisational capabilities and leadership.

'Interests which are linked to the profession should be included. So, if I have somebody apply for a marketing job, I would like to know whether they are involved with any professional bodies, whether they have participated in international conferences and whether they have written any articles. This is very important because it shows that it is not only a job that they are looking for, it's much more than that; it's a passion, it's something they believe in, it's really their career. '

Adrian Cojocaru at Mars Drinks

With respect to graduate or entry-level job seekers, this section will probably say quite a lot about you and it would advantageous to include. Specify interests that highlight teamwork, leadership skills, drive and enthusiasm. Keep this section short and where possible, relevant to your target position.

5. Extra-curricular activities

Express any additional responsibilities you hold on a personal level, for example, fund-raising for the PTA.

EXAMPLES – ADDITIONAL INFORMATION

Example 1:

Driving Licence:	*Full*
Location:	*Willing to travel*
Interests:	*Enjoy technology, keeping up-to-date with financial affairs, skiing and spending time with family*

Example 2:

Security Clearance:	*Cleared to SC Level*
Location:	*Willing to relocate*
Interests:	*Web design, socialising and keeping fit*

Tip

- This section can also be headed 'Extra Curricular Activities'.
- If you are short of space, you can summarise your computer and languages skills here too.
- Include only information that will be supportive to your application or enhance your chances of being invited to interview.

Take a few moments now to compile this section.

CHAPTER 19

REFERENCES

Providing references on your CV is an area of contention. Most agree that references are something that should be taken up once you have been offered the job. Unless you are explicitly requested to provide them, omit them from your CV. It is reputed that providing references is inappropriate and unprofessional.

> ❝ 34% of employers do not want references on a CV,
> 30% do want a reference and 36% had no preference. ❞
>
> *CMC Survey 2007*

As 34% do not want to see references on a CV and 36% are indifferent, that could technically equate to 70% being against references.

The risk of providing references is that there is nothing to stop a prospective employer contacting your current or previous employer. It would be very embarrassing and very harmful if they contacted your current employer who is likely to be quite unaware that you are in the market for a new job.

The normal process is that references are taken up once a job offer is received and this is when they should be provided. The benefit to providing references at offer stage is that you have time to request permission from your referees and are also able to brief them on the position and the skills required to perform the job.

It is quite acceptable, space permitting, to put 'references available on request'.

CHAPTER 20

FORMAT, STRUCTURE AND PRESENTATION

Having followed Chapters 1 through to 19, you should have produced all the content that you need to prepare your impressive CV. The next step is to clarify the order in which to present the information and gain an insight into how to best present the information visually, as first impressions really do count.

> *You never get a second chance to make a first impression.*
>
> *Matt Lauer*

CV writing is an art form but art can be copied. The art is to include enough information to keep your audience captivated but at the same time not to provide too much detail, so as to lose their interest.

> *CVs are sales documents; they should leave the reader wanting more. If you give the whole story, people will make a view – they will make a judgement, maybe the right one, maybe the wrong one.*
>
> *Giles Crewdson at Korn Ferry*

The consensus of all those interviewed is that a CV should be clear, concise, focused, well structured and easy to read.

This chapter covers how to effectively lay out and present the information, and concludes with discussing the body of your CV.

In conjunction with reviewing the information below, revert to the CD to review various templates and examples, which will prove invaluable when preparing the first draft of your CV.

LAYOUT

Information needs to be presented in:

- **The correct order,** i.e. most important information first.
  This will vary depending on your level of experience and what you are looking to emphasise. Generally, those with less than two years' work experience will look to highlight their education as this will be of most interest to a potential employer. Those with more experience will look to highlight their achievements, areas of expertise and employment history. As mentioned in individual chapters, if you are applying for a specific job and need to draw attention to maybe your technical expertise or language skills, these should be presented on page one of your CV.

Your CV may need to be tweaked depending on the role being applied for.

- **Reverse chronological order,** i.e. most recent first.
  Do not begin your CV with information that is out of date, i.e. qualifications completed in 1975.

Finally, do not be tempted to write your CV as a story as this makes your CV difficult to read.

The sequence in which information is presented will depend largely on your level. The next four pages consist of two documents: the first two pages detail the order in which to present the information if you have less than two years' experience. The next document is relevant to those with more than two years' experience. These are to serve as a guideline only.

Layout – Less than two years' work experience

Page 1

Name
Contact information

CAREER OBJECTIVE

PROFILE STATEMENT

KEY STRENGTHS

EDUCATION AND TRAINING

ACHIEVEMENTS

Leadership

Scholarships and Awards

Page 2

WORK EXPERIENCE

VOLUNTARY WORK

PROFESSIONAL ASSOCIATIONS

PUBLICATIONS/PATENTS

COMPUTER SKILLS

LANGUAGES

ADDITIONAL INFORMATION

Driving Licence:
Location:
Interests and Hobbies:

If you have space at the end of page one, your work history can commence there.

Layout – More than two years' work experience

Page 1

Name
Contact information

CAREER OBJECTIVE

PROFESSIONAL PROFILE

KEY SKILLS

KEY ACHIEVEMENTS

EMPLOYMENT HISTORY

Page 2

EMPLOYMENT HISTORY CONTINUED

VOLUNTARY WORK

PROFESSIONAL ASSOCIATIONS

PUBLICATIONS/PATENTS

COMPUTER SKILLS

LANGUAGES

EDUCATION AND TRAINING

ADDITIONAL INFORMATION

Driving Licence:
Location:
Interests and Hobbies:

PRESENTATION

The importance of presenting your content well should not be underestimated. The 'look and feel' of a CV can be more important than the content itself and you need to make sure you get it right. You could have the best CV in the world but if it is not reader friendly and appealing to the eye, it could make its way to the 'maybe' pile or even the bin.

1. Font type and size

The most acceptable font types are Arial or Times New Roman. It is tempting to use something different because there are many interesting fonts like Verdana, Tahoma and Comic Sans, and people feel using something unique will help them stand out. Unfortunately, the reality is that Arial or Times New Roman are the most reader-friendly and as such, the preferred choice of most recruitment professionals. Do not be enticed into using anything else.

With regards the font size, we are so conscious of filling up two pages that if our CV is only one and half pages, we are temped to increase the font size to 14 points. Conversely, if we are unable to get our CV onto two pages, we are tempted to reduce the font size to 8 or 9 points. In the first scenario, your CV becomes unprofessional looking if the font size is too large. In the second scenario, if it is too small, it is likely to be overlooked.

What is the best font size? It is recommended that you use a font size of 12-points if using Times New Roman, although a font size of 11-points is acceptable. If using Arial, 11-points is ideal but 10-points is suitable. Use font size 18 or 20-point for your name.

Tip

- **Use Arial or Times New Roman.**
- **Keep font size consistent throughout.**
- **Contemplate a three-page CV if you are unable to fit your CV into two-pages. Conversely, have a one page CV if you have nothing more to say.**

---

2. Bold and italics

Use italic and bold to highlight certain areas or key points, but use sparingly. Too much of something can become over-bearing and can appear arrogant.

3. White space

To ensure that your document is appealing to the eye, utilise lots of white space and allow for generous margins of at least 2.5cms on the right and left hand sides, and 2.1cms top and bottom.

4. Consistency

- Keep spacing even – if you decide on one line between each heading, keep this consistent throughout.
- If you select a particular font type and size, keep with the same font type and size throughout your CV.
- Ensure all dates line up on either the right or left hand side.
- Keep style consistent, for example, if you opt to have your job titles in italics and your company name is capitalised, keep with this format throughout your CV.

5. Bullet points

Utilise bullet points throughout your CV; this makes your CV punchy and easy to read. The exception is your career objective and profile statements, and any areas that may consist of just a few lines or sentences, for example 'languages' or 'professional affiliations'.

6. Complex formatting

As with using fancy fonts, it is tempting to use colour, borders, shading, decorative lines and graphics as people often believe that this will help them to stand out. This is the exception rather than the norm. Simple is best. Avoid using complex formatting as it does not read well and more often than not, it does not scan, email or fax well.

7. Headings

Utilising headings makes your CV look clean, reader friendly and easy to follow. Keep your headings consistent in appearance, i.e. same font and size, and place them in capitals and bold.

8. Spelling and grammar

Spelling mistakes, poor grammar and typos in CVs are surprisingly common and were a bug bear by all experts interviewed. It is not only foreigners whose first language is not English who slip up here, too often it is senior executives. Spelling and grammatical areas show a lack of attention to detail and it is often a simple error like this that can land your CV in the bin without any further consideration. Do not rely on spell-check as it is not perfect. Double and triple check your document and then get someone you trust to do the same. Often, you do not pick up your own mistakes.

Two of the experts had this to say:

> *I would never ever expect to see a typo in a CV; I want to put them in the bin.*
>
> *[Typos say] something about the person and their attention to detail.*
>
> Anna Tomkins at Vodafone

> *Poor grammar and spelling mistakes are always disappointing with all the tools available, we would hope people could format sentences and get the spelling right. We're looking for people with really good attention to detail; if people can't show that on their CV, then to me it is a downfall from the start.*
>
> Leila Bliss at KPMG

If English is not your first language, find a company that will proofread your document for a small fee or approach a professional CV writing business and ask for their help. A spelling mistake or typo can be one of the most serious mistakes you can make on your CV and can be your downfall.

9. Format

Most employers still prefer to receive a CV in Word format. Avoid using Word Pad (RTF files) as not all organisations can open these files. Adobe PDF always looks good; the beauty with a PDF is that the formatting you see will be the same someone else sees (which is not always the case with Word). Not all companies can open PDF files and not all agencies can scan them. Should you wish to send a PDF file, contact the company first to establish whether they can read PDF files.

10. Hardcopies

Nowadays, most companies expect you to email your document or apply online. If you decide to send a hardcopy, ensure your CV and cover letter are laser-printed on high quality paper (120 gram) and it is recommended that you send a softcopy too. When posting your CV, do not fold or staple your document.

> *64% of respondents preferred to receive CVs via email.*
>
> *CMC Survey 2007*

Tip

When emailing your CV and cover letter, make sure you pay as much attention to your email as you did to your CV. If you create a bad impression here, your documents may never be opened.

Summary

Your CV is your marketing document and says a lot about you as an individual. If the content has been poorly presented in any way, you can be assured that the prospective employer will build an image of you in their mind and will make a judgement, rightly or wrongly, about you as a prospective employee.

All of the experts interviewed stressed how important good formatting is. Below are some important tips:

- keep it simple;
- use bullet points throughout;
- avoid gimmicks, logos, colour and fancy fonts;
- keep it organised;
- ensure the layout is easy on the eye;
- all dates should line up;
- fonts type and size should be consistent;
- do not overuse bold;
- use headings;
- avoid producing a monologue.

> *I've seen CVs that have literally been a monologue; how are you meant to pull out the key information?*
>
> Louise Mayo at KPMG

STRUCTURE

This section covers how to structure the information and discusses the ideal CV length.

Selling points

Ensure that key points jump out on your CV.

> *You shouldn't make the reviewer work too hard to find your crown jewels; if you have three or four key selling points, whatever they might happen to be, it's imperative to make sure that those are very much in evidence on the page.*
>
> Jonathan Jones at Goldman Sachs

Keep your target audience in mind when writing your CV as selling points may vary depending on the role being applied for.

> *People need to adjust their message depending on the role or the company. Be very focused on whom you are targeting and deliver on the target.*
>
> Adrian Cojocaru at Mars Drinks

Sentences and paragraphs
- Sentences need to be kept short and punchy, making it easy to read. Vary your sentence length and keep sentences to no more than 15 words.
- Do not use three words when one will do.
- Keep paragraphs to no longer than four lines.
- Begin sentences with action words and phrases as per table at the end of this book.

Language

- CVs should always be written in the first person, for example, 'I have' rather than 'he has'. Ideally the 'I' should be omitted altogether.
- Avoid jargon unless you work in a highly technical field. Bear in mind, decision makers are often HR personnel and they may not have a strong technical understanding. Your CV needs to appeal to the widest possible audience.
- Do not include job titles and company specific jargon that will not be understood outside of your company.
- Utilise short and simple words without sounding infantile. Stay away from obscure words.
- It is advisable not to use abbreviations in your CV unless you are expressing your education or professional affiliations.
- Vary your words and phrases as repetition reduces the impact of your CV.

CV Length

The length of your CV is largely dependent on your target audience but it is most widely accepted that a CV should not exceed two pages.

> *72% of HR Specialists believe that a CV should be no more than two pages long.*
>
> *CMC Survey 2007*

Technical CVs, academic CVs or those with very lengthy careers are the exception and can extend to three pages.

On the whole, the industry experts interviewed agreed with the two page rule.

> *One of the things I do tend to tell people is if you want to use a multi-page format that's okay but you had better make sure that page one is good enough that people have an appetite to get to page two and page three.*
>
> *Jonathan Jones at Goldman Sachs*

> ' *The ideal length is a top copy plus two pages. The top page summarises who you are very briefly in a way that's designed for your reader and then the following two pages are generic. [Will later describes the top copy as a cover letter.]* '
>
> Will Dawkins at Odgers Ray and Berndtson

> ' *Two pages are more than enough because you can sell yourself at the interview. Some people will send four, five, six pages and by the time you get to the end you're not in a very happy mood.* '
>
> Sean Jowell at KPMG

Two of the experts interviewed felt that one page would be ideal and had this to say:

> ' *Two pages are ideal, although if it could fit on to one page, even better. What is important is the quality of the information.* '
>
> Adrian Cojocaru at Mars Drinks

> ' *More is less. If you are speaking to people who have an understanding of the industry that you have worked in, [providing a lot of detail] can be patronising to the reader.* '
>
> Giles Crewdsen at Korn Ferry

Tip

- **Divide information into clear, easy to read sections. The use of headings is important.**
- **Place the most important information on the first page.**
- **Provide enough information to whet the reader's appetite and ensure that you leave them wanting more.**
- **Keep the information structured, concise and relevant.**

With the above in mind, select a template from the appended CD and begin slotting your notes into the document. After you have completed your CV, read through this section again to ensure you have adhered to all the rules and refer to Chapter 22 for top CV tips.

CHAPTER 21

REVIEWING REAL CVS

This chapter provides examples of CVs from real people, each of whom was receiving a poor response to their CV. The examples provided cover a variety of industries and include people at different stages in their career.

Reading through each individual's original CV and the detailed commentary will help you identify common mistakes and point out 'how not' to write a CV. In each instance, the revised/professionally reformatted CV that went on to win numerous interviews is provided.

Example 1: Adam Green
Adam is a management consultant and project manager with over 20 years' project management experience in the financial services sector, and is seeking to secure the same.

Example 2: Andrea Smith
Andrea is a highly qualified graduate with a Bachelor of Science degree, an MBA and a diploma in Legal Practice. She is a first-time job seeker seeking to secure a graduate position, ideally with a consultancy.

Example 3: Rob Brown
Rob is a senior test analyst with nine years' commercial experience gained in the telecommunications sector.

Example 4: James Black
James is a software engineer and solutions designer with 10 years' experience of both public and private sector contracts.

Example 5: Poncho Devaga
Poncho is a sales professional seeking to utilise his skills and experience in leisure, advertising and engineering sales, to secure a position in the aerospace industry.

Example 6: Alan Jones
Alan is a senior manager with 20+ years' experience in operations, manufacturing and in the deployment of major production initiatives.

Example 7: Jess Graham
Jess works part-time as a cash officer administrator. She was seeking to draw on previous marketing experience and various marketing qualifications to secure a role as a marketer in the financial services industry.

Adam Green

2 No Name Street, London SW2
Tel: 0123 456 789 (office) Mobile: 07123 456 789

Following extensive experience as a process improvement, project and line manager in the Financial Services sector, Adam has over 5 years experience as a consultant. Adam has worked with a wide range of organisations helping them to develop and implement a strategic approach to continuous improvement and a practical deployment of this to deliver results. He has experience of a wide range of improvement tools including process and performance management and improvement, EFQM, amongst others.

Special skills and expertise
- Business Process Modelling / Reengineering
- Process Improvement
- Application of Information technology, systems and web based technology
- Project Management
- Excellent general consultancy skills, able to facilitate large workshops.
- Business Analysis
- Strategy planning

Career History
Adam worked in the Retail Banking Financial Services industry for 24 years gaining promotion to senior management and performing a number of line management, process improvement and project management roles. Adam developed and implemented strategies to move a large operations centre from an "order taking" culture to a world-class service oriented profit centre. Adam's skills in developing high performing teams and rapid effective change approaches were deployed in a number of key projects including the relocation of a major call centre, the centralisation and the design, development and implementation of information systems for the processing of financial products. Adam gained considerable practical experience implementing successful Business Excellence approaches in an organisation that became a finalist in the UK Business Excellence award 1999.

Since becoming a consultant in 2000 major consulting assignments include:
- An intensive business process re-engineering assignment for a major Corporation that identified significant opportunities to rationalise costs while maintaining levels of customer satisfaction.
- A series of assignments with several major public bodies and public limited companies to enable them to improve their critical business processes including Benchmarking and the application of the Business Excellence model to the supplier process.
- A series of assignments to develop key business processes and design, build and implement web based process management system in 2 major public bodies and a Local Authority.
- Designing, building and implementing a web based Process model of the Offender Management Process in the Criminal Justice Sector
- Putting together successful bids and tenders for consultancy work.

Professional Qualifications and Memberships
- Associate of the Chartered Institute of Bankers (ACIB)
- Cranfield School of management (Business Operations Certificate)
- Ashridge Strategic Management Development Centre. (Strategic Decisions Alumni)
- UKQA Assessor
- Professional Contractors Group

Commentary – Adam Green

- **HEADING** – Adam's CV has been correctly headed with his name and contact details.

- **VISUAL LAYOUT** – There is good use of white space, and Adam's general layout is fine.

- **STRUCTURE** – Under Career History, Adam's sentence and paragraph length are too long. Sentences should be short and punchy, and should generally not exceed 15 words. Paragraphs should be no more than four lines, making it easy and quick to read.

- **LENGTH** – A CV should generally be two pages in length. Adam's CV is little bit short on information and does not provide an employer with enough information on which to base a decision.

- **ENGLISH LANGUAGE** – Adam's command of the English language is good and there are no spelling or grammatical errors. He has, however, written his CV in the third person; CVs should always be written in the first person, i.e. 'I have' rather than 'he has', although it is recommended that the 'I' be omitted altogether.

- **PROFILE** – Importantly he has included a profile, but it does little to sell Adam's skills and experience. More emphasis should be placed on Adam's key experience, skills, achievements and motivations.

- **KEY SKILLS** – This section is good and should be retained, but Adam should perhaps expand on each skill, providing a brief overview of where he has demonstrated each of these skills.

- **EMPLOYMENT HISTORY** – Adam's work history is not very reader-friendly and should be broken down into sections. Adam needs to include the names of the companies he has worked for and his job titles. Additionally, he should provide detail of the last 10 years of his work history, with emphasis being placed on the last five. In each role he should emphasise how his employer has benefited from his work and where appropriate, he must quantify his achievements.

- **ACHIEVEMENTS** – As it is important to shout about your achievements, Adam should include a separate 'Achievements' section where he can highlight between three and five of his major achievements. As mentioned in previous sections of this book, an employer needs to know why they should employ you. They are interested in what you can bring to their organisation, how you can solve their problems and what the potential benefit to hiring you will be. It is important that this is conveyed in a CV rather than just listing a fact.

- **EDUCATIONAL HISTORY** – Adam has not included details of his highest educational qualifications, which potential employers may want to see.

- **COMPUTER SKILLS** – There is no mention of IT skills. As it is increasingly prevalent in most industries, it is vital that he includes his proficiency with various packages and programmes.

Conclusion

Adam's CV has some good content but it is a little short on information. Information on earlier roles should be provided together with detail of what he achieved in each of his positions. Additionally, he failed to include 'Achievements' and 'Education' sections. In summary, he needs to expand on the information already provided.

On the following two pages, you will find Adam's revised CV, which was professionally reformatted. Shortly after sending his CV to prospective employers, he received several positive comments about his CV and a very good job offer, which he accepted. The quality of his CV was cited as one of his main strengths during the selection process.

REVISED CV – ADAM GREEN

Adam Green

2 No Name Street, London SW2
Tel (h): 0123 456 789 Tel (m): 07123 456 789
Email: adamgreen@abcd.com

PROFESSIONAL PROFILE

A proactive, self-reliant and highly skilled **Project Manager** with an outstanding track record of achievement in both Project Management and Consultancy, gained across a variety of industries. With 24 years' experience in the Financial Services sector in a number of line management, process improvement and project management roles, possesses a broad understanding of the industry and the full project life cycle. Thrives on developing and implementing a strategic approach to continuous improvement and for designing systems to rationalise costs and improve processes.

Excellent communication, organisation, planning and problem solving skills, coupled with extensive experience of a wide range of improvement tools including process, performance management, and EFQM (European Foundation for Quality Management). Demonstrates an ability to rapidly assimilate, simplify and understand large amounts of company information and use this information to provide new insights, uncover issues and identify targets for improvement. Recognised as intelligent, adaptable, supportive and good-humoured with an innate ability to stay calm under pressure. Passionate about delivering benefits and exceeding customer expectations.

AREAS OF EXPERTISE

- **Project Management** – Extensive experience of managing projects to enable companies to improve their critical business processes
- **Consultancy** – Thorough understanding of internal and external consulting including Benchmarking and applying the Business Excellence model
- **Business Process Modelling/Re-engineering** – A performance record of defining and significantly improving processes, and leading overall change management programmes from scratch, incorporating change into organisations
- **Application of IT, Systems and Web-Based Technology** – In-depth knowledge of defining and specifying requirements, building, and implementing new IT systems. Experience of applying web technology to the delivery of process modelling work
- **Business Analysis** – A talent for reviewing key drivers in an organisation and utilising the Business Excellence model to access an organisation's capability in depth, including KPIs and elements that affect bottom-line
- **Strategy Planning** – Developed business plans for a business unit within an organisation, and have completed a Strategic Decision Course

CAREER HIGHLIGHTS

- Lead Consultant involved in the design, build and implementation of a web-based process model for the Offender Management Process in the Criminal Justice Sector. This ongoing project is in the process of being piloted in two prisons and national probation areas. Long-term, there would be a significant reduction in re-offending rates and more effective compliance with procedures and processes
- Effectively managed the design, build and implementation of a web-based process model for XYZ Agency and captured 'the knowledge', which involved designing and running numerous workshops across the country for the client
- Successfully project managed the relocation of a major call centre for ABC Bank, bringing together IT and Telecoms, HR, Process Modelling, Design, and Customer Service functions. The project involved closing down a business in one location and re-opening it in another, and successfully integrating the old business into the new. This 18-month project, involved managing a team of 25 and a budget of £3m
- Project managed a centralisation project, which involved building from scratch the capability to operate centrally and setting up a programme to migrate the work from the network to the centre, without disrupting the service. This project involved the management of 60+ people, and was completed on time and to budget (£3m)

PROFESSIONAL EXPERIENCE

OPQ PLC: Leeds   **2000–Date**

Management Consultant

- Frequently meet with clients to comprehend the requirements of the work and to gain a thorough understanding of the organisation. Assignments typically include uncovering problems, managing change initiatives, coaching, training and stakeholder management
- Applying the Business Excellence model to review the supply chain of the XYZ Agency to access the quality and capability of their suppliers in the long-term
- A key player in an intensive business process re-engineering assignment for MRQ plc that identified significant opportunities to rationalise costs while maintaining levels of customer satisfaction; a project which saved the company £3.1m
- Delivered an assignment for the XYZ Agency involving the implementation of Lean Techniques in Procurement using a tool kit of lean six sigma tools and techniques. Together with two colleagues, identified opportunities to reduce overall procurement time by 66%
- Project managed end-to-end e-Business Management Systems for XYZ Agency, NPL Ltd, and GTY Ltd. Developed the process standards to be used throughout the work; ran workshops; designed, built and populated the software tool used to publish the process models; and developed close working relationships with technical teams involved in implementing the tool
- Organised and managed several bids and tenders for consultancy work. Won bids ranging from £50k to £1m+, some of which included the NPL Ltd, STR District Council and DEF CC
- Improved AMT plc's bid process through applying the Business Excellence Model; secured an IT services contract and the building of schools contract, worth £20m+ each

ABC BANK PLC: Various Locations   **1976–2000**

Project Manager   **1995–2000**

- Set up and managed a Business Excellence department consisting of 12 staff, to maintain business excellence within a major contact centre consisting of over 700 staff. Managed a series of assignments including business planning, business improvements, training, and customer satisfaction surveys/feedback
- Reviewed the organisation's KPIs and made recommendations. Following the adoption of suggestions, devised a key performance pack of measures and a balanced score card
- Managed a programme that developed and implemented strategies to move a large operations centre from an 'order taking' culture to a 'world-class service oriented profit centre'. The programme significantly improved customer feedback scores, secured more business, and improved cross-sales
- Developed several high performing teams and rapid effective change approaches to various projects including the relocation of a major call centre; the centralisation, design, development and implementation of IT systems for the processing of financial products
- Gained considerable experience implementing successful Business Excellence approaches in a company that was a finalist in the UK Business Excellence award 19XX

Productivity Services Consultant and Senior Consultant   **1990–1995**

Various roles in the Branch Network, including Securities and Lending   **1976–1990**

COMPUTER SKILLS

- High level of competence in the field of web-based technology, MS Project, Dreamweaver, Photoshop, HTML and CSS (intermediate)
- Proficient user of Microsoft Office – Word, Excel, PowerPoint, Access and Outlook

EDUCATION AND PROFESSIONAL DEVELOPMENT

UK Quality Award Assessor Training: British Quality Foundation   2000

Strategic Decisions Programme: Ashridge Strategic
  Management Development Centre   2000

Business Operations Certificate: Cranfield School of management   1990

Associate Chartered Institute of Bankers (ACIB)   1982
8 'O' Levels

Interests: Builds and maintains PCs and office networks

Ms Andrea Smith
Curriculum Vitae

Address: 3 No Name Street
Manchester
WA1

Telephone: 07123 456 789

Email: andrea.smith@abcd.co.uk

CAREER INTENTIONS

As a student living and studying in the UK I have learnt to self-motivate and manage my life to successfully achieve my goals. With excellent business and language skills, I am looking to enter a challenging graduate position in general business, ideally within a consultancy role.

KEY SKILLS

- **Leadership and Teamwork:** At ABS, I successfully organised and took part in research projects for a number of international companies.
- **Analytical:** Throughout my studies I have successfully honed skills of independent thought and analysis. Utilising these skills, I evaluated and developed a financial strategy for the 'XYZ Child' foundation.
- **Problem-solving:** Whilst studying towards my MBA, I designed an 'X-efficiency' program for a company, thereby helping to increase their profit.
- **Business acumen:** I am a keen reader of business publications and have been involved in setting up a business society for Romanian students at Manchester University.
- **Languages:** Romanian (native) Russian (fluent) English (fluent) Spanish (intermediate) French (basic)

EDUCATION AND DISTINCTIONS

Current	**MSc in European Studies (due to complete in Sep 2008)** Manchester Business School, London, UK
Sep 2007	**Postgraduate Diploma in Legal Practice** University of Westminster, London, UK
Jan 2007	**MBA in International Business and Finance (Distinction)** Brunel University, Middlesex, UK
Dec 2005	**BA LW (Hons) in Law and Business Management, 2:1 (top 10%)** Middlesex University, Middlesex, UK
Sep 2002	**Foundation Diploma in Liberal Arts** **Law (A), Politics and Society (A), Intercultural Communication (A), Communication Skills (A), Thinking Critically (A), Business Studies (B+)** Middlesex University, Middlesex, UK
Jun 2000	**13 GCSEs (Overall grade A*), Graduated with Honours** Secondary School, Romania

CAREER HISTORY

Apr 2005 – Jan 2006   **Marketing Research Assistant, Communicator and Assistant Team-Leader**
ABS, Manchester, UK

- Collection of data from customers, analysis and preparation of data
- Communicating with customers on the telephone, handling queries and complaints

VOLUNTARY WORK EXPERIENCE

Aug 2005 – Present   **Volunteer**
XYZ Child Foundation, Romania

Most of my work, done through the internet and during academic holidays, involves:

- Assisting Romanian volunteers with the translation of medical and other documents, and negotiating with local officials and sponsors
- Involvement in the charity's educational program for children

Aug 2006 – Sep 2007   **Adviser**
DGH Advice Bureau, Manchester,UK

- Advising people on a number of social policy issues including EU legislation, housing and immigration policies, discrimination, benefit and debt collection

ACHIEVEMENTS

- Whilst working at ABS, I was awarded 'Best Performance of the Month'.
- In 2001 I was chosen to represent the UK at the Global Young Leaders Conference, based on my leadership potential and academic excellence.
- In 1998, I was made captain of the Romanian National Tennis Team.

INTERESTS & ACTIVITIES

Continuous learning is important to me, hence I am currently learning to speak French and Spanish. A regular reader of 'The Economist' and 'New Law Journal', I also enjoy reading Russian literature and Greek philosophy. As a keen traveller, I have visited over 15 countries in Europe, the USA and the Americas.

REFEREES

Dr J Jones
Manchester Business School
Houghton Street
London WC2A

Tel: 020 1234 5678

Mr A Adams
Charity Manager
XYZ Child Foundation
20 Central Street
Zaporozhye, Romania

Tel: +381234567891

Commentary – Andrea Smith

- **HEADING** – Andrea's CV includes a title/heading, which is not necessary as it should be obvious what the document is. Her CV should be headed with just her name and contact details.

- **VISUAL LAYOUT** – Prospective employers prefer a simple layout as it is more reader-friendly. Moreover, complex formatting involving borders and shading, is not conducive to being faxed, copied or scanned and vital information may be lost as a result.

- **LENGTH** – At two pages, the length of her CV is perfect.

- **STRUCTURE** – The overall structure of Andrea's CV is good. Sentences and paragraphs are a good length, and all information has been presented in the correct order.

- **ENGLISH LANGUAGE** – Her use of the English language is good and there are no spelling mistakes or grammatical errors.

- **PROFILE** – Andrea has not included a profile, which is a useful sales tool. She needs to summarise her background, skills, achievements and motivations, whilst also conveying a little about her personality.

- **OBJECTIVE** – Her career objective has been captured well and should be retained.

- **KEY SKILLS** – This section is good and should remain.

- **EDUCATIONAL HISTORY** – Her educational history has been expressed well.

- **EMPLOYMENT HISTORY** – This section is a little lean and does not provide an employer with enough information. She needs to express what skills she has gained and any achievements or benefits her work has had for an organisation.

- **ACHIEVEMENTS** – It is important to include this section early on in the CV and hence, it should be brought forward to the first page or the top of the second. It is also important to include any achievements at school or university as this provides a prospective employer with an insight into who you are and what your potential is.

- **COMPUTER SKILLS** – There is no mention of IT skills. As it is increasingly important to be computer literate, it is important that Andrea details her proficiency with various packages and systems.

- **REFERRALS** – Referees should not be included on a CV; it is considered inappropriate and unprofessional to include them. Andrea can, however, state that 'references are available on request'.

Conclusion

Andrea's CV has some good content, being her educational history and her key skills sections. In order to ensure that her CV best represents her skills and experience, and provides a prospective employer with an insight into what she can bring to their organisation, Andrea needs to provide a summary of her skills and background in the form of a profile statement. She should also provide detail of what she has achieved at school, university and during work experience, and needs to expand on skills gained or learnt during her work experience. It is also imperative that she amends her layout, ensuring that her information is presented as simply as possible.

Andrea's CV, which was professionally reformatted, can be found on the subsequent two pages. She was invited to four interviews out of five applications made.

REVISED CV – ANDREA SMITH

Andrea Smith

3 No Name Street, Manchester WA1

Tel (m): 07123 456 789

Email: andrea.smith@abcd.co.uk

PROFILE & OBJECTIVE

A highly self-motivated, ambitious and determined graduate of Law and Business Management, with a Diploma in Legal Practice and an MBA in International Business and Finance. Currently studying towards a Masters degree in European Studies.

Highly focused, rational and open-minded with valuable work experience within a variety of commercial environments. Well-defined communication and interpersonal skills, diplomatic and good-humoured, maintaining a positive and supportive attitude with the ability to achieve desired results. Works well under pressure and excels in planning and organisation.

With excellent business and language skills, and a desire to achieve significant results, is seeking to secure a challenging graduate position in general business, ideally within a consultancy role.

KEY SKILLS

- **Problem Solving** – Creative, logical and lateral thinker
- **Leadership** – Strong motivational skills with the ability to enthuse staff
- **Research & Analytical** – Practical research experience, interpreting evidence and information
- **Communication & Interpersonal** – Excellent oral, written and listening skills at all levels
- **Interpersonal** – Able to interact within a group, encouraging input from others to reach a decision through compromise
- **Organisation & Time Management** – Prioritises, schedules and coordinates workload, able to multi-task and manage time effectively
- **Administrative Management** – Writing and drafting of documentation, maintaining accurate records
- **Relationship Management** – Deals effectively at all levels with clients and colleagues
- **Problem Solving** – Acts quickly and efficiently to resolve unexpected difficulties
- **IT** – Proficient user of Word, Excel, PowerPoint and InfoPath

ACHIEVEMENTS

- Set up a Business Society for Romanian Students at Manchester University.
- Led a small project team at ABS, to conduct a market research survey for ERG Limited. Recorded the team's performance and ensured all data was correctly entered into the online database accurately. Exceeded targets and collected information from over 1000 customers over a two-week period. Successfully motivated the team with a reward voucher for the highest performing individual.
- Displayed entrepreneurial flair and business acumen in 2006, providing assistance to a friend investigating the option of opening a fast-food franchise in Latvia. Performed a PESTLE and SWOT analysis and established a USP for the business. Created a business plan which successfully secured funding in the form of a business loan from a state-run financial institution. The company is now growing profitably, following its first year of trading.

- Conducted an external and internal analysis of a local Romanian business in 2006/2007, which was experiencing decline and subsequently developed an x-efficiency cost-cutting programme. Created and implemented improved debt collecting and investment strategies and negotiated mutually rewarding agreements with the company's suppliers and wholesalers. Resulted in a significant increase in profitability (around 25%) and no staff redundancies were necessary.
- Received the 'Employee of the Month' award at ABS in 2005, in recognition of enhanced performance.
- Selected in 2001 to represent the UK at the Global Young Leaders Conference in the USA, based upon demonstrable leadership potential and academic excellence displayed whilst at Manchester University.

EDUCATION

MSc in European Studies, Manchester University (to complete in Sept 2008)
Postgraduate Diploma in Legal Practice, University of Westminster, 2007
MBA in International Business & Finance (Distinction), Brunel University, 2007
2.1 BA (Hons) Degree in Law & Business Management, Middlesex University, 2005
Foundation Diploma in Liberal Arts, Middlesex University, 2002
13 GCSEs, (Overall grade A*), Graduated with Honours, Romania

WORK EXPERIENCE

Apr'05–Jan'06   ABS, Thame
Market Research Assistant/Assistance Team Leader

- Worked with FTSE 100 and FTSE 250 client companies at ABS including STP, YZW Limited and KLI plc.
- Frequently tasked with the role of data interpretation and analysis.
- Collected, analysed and prepared data for reports.
- Assisted in the drafting of questionnaires for use in focus groups.

VOLUNTARY WORK

Aug'06–Sept'07   DGH Advice Bureau, Manchester

- Provided advice on a number of social policy issues including EU legislation, housing, immigration, discrimination, benefits and debt collection.

Aug'05–Present   XYZ Child Foundation, Romania

- Provide support through the internet and during academic holidays, assisting with translation of documents and negotiating with local officials and sponsors.
- Assist with the educational programme for children.
- Evaluated and developed a financial strategy for the foundation.
- Received a donation of £25,000 from a previous employer for 'XYZ Child Foundation'.

LANGUAGE SKILLS

Fluent in English, Romanian (native), Russian, Spanish (intermediate) with basic skills in French.

INTERESTS

Travel – visited over 15 countries in Europe and the USA
Regular reader of 'The Economist' and 'New Law Journal'
Enjoy Russian literature and Greek philosophy
Tennis – won The Women's Tennis Romanian Championships in 1998

References available on request

Rob Brown
3 No Name Close, London SW1
(Mobile) 07123 456 789 rbrown@abcd.com

Professional Summary:

An experienced test analyst within the telecommunications market sector with full project lifecycle and key testing skills. I'm results-orientated and quality-focused. I have extensive experience in testing Universal Voice Messaging Systems and Fixed Line Short Messaging System applications, providing second line and On-Call support. I have strong leadership skills and perform effectively in pressurised working environments. I have high levels of motivation and perform well both on my own and as part of a team.

Career History:

January 2003 to Present
Test Analyst
- Responsible for all aspects of end-to-end management of testing for key projects.
- Appointed to undertake configuration & benchmark testbed & live test lifecycles.
- Included hw & sw installations & upgrades plus parallel adherence to project dates.
- Drove pro-active instigation of capacity planning, producing performance metrics.
- Scheduled and delivered day-to-day key VMSC real-time & out-of-hours support.
- Combined above with pertinent systems administration for top quality user service.
- Managed regular review & production of technical specifications & test documents.
- Prime instigator of re-build & new configuration of unified messaging within testbed
- Influential team member for comprehensive test preparation.
- Responsible for all elements of complex business, systems and integration testing.
- Appointed to define & execute all test activities, including training & documentation
- Covered various stages in the testing life cycle to include component, system (functional & non-functional) integration & UAT testing
- Created and executed test scripts and plans over widespread functions for clients
- Involved full test lifecycle for customised voicemail & unified messaging systems
- Undertook major tester role for key staged delivery of XYZ 'Premium' project
- Became member of the out of hours XYZ client support group providing rapid solutions that occur on client live system.
- Comprised rapid fault diagnosis & resolution for customer problems as they occur
- Controlled co-ordination of testing across all components for major XYZ projects.
- Investigating Unisys program failures through debugging and assisting with the development of corrections.

September 2002 to January 2003
Operations Shift Leader
- Responsible for problem/change management for Unisys Mainframes in live and test environments.
- Responsible for all elements of comprehensive Voicemail System Service activities
- Managed a 4 man shift making sure all operational duties are carried out and maintained
- Support shift members and set objectives ensuring that their targets are achievable and can be exceeded
- Producing and maintaining general operational procedures in conjunction with service review requirements.

September 1999 to January 2002
Shift Operator

- Assessing schemes using the Quality Assessment Framework.
- Appointed to plan and deliver ongoing operational support to extensive client base
- Ensured provision of timely & high-quality service deliverables to 6,000000+ users.
- Reconciled and prioritised ad-hoc customer queries & faults with daily scheduling
- Incorporated hw & sw application support, with installation & configuration
- Ensured repeated quality delivery against combined internal & external objectives
- Supporting applications in a Unisys Clearpath MCP operating environment.
- Administering and maintaining the Unisys Clearpath application product parameter and configuration files.
- Performing daily, weekly and monthly systems back-ups and database dumps.
- Conducting console operations and monitoring for Unisys A-Series and Clearpath systems in a 7x24x365 consolidated Data Centre environment.
- Observing multiple monitor screens for alerts, alarms and indicators of abnormal processing for the Unisys Systems.
- Performing Software and Hardware upgrades, installations and full testing of the Unisys Mainframes.
- Experience in online and batch programming using Unisys COBOL, Enterprise Database Server (DMSII), WFL, CANDE and Transaction Server (COMS).

Professional:

- Various in-house & external training programmes
- Effective communication & presentation skills
- Team leadership & motivation techniques
- Hardware platforms include Unisys NX5600, NX4800
- OS Software applications include GPM, Linux, Unisys A-Series
- MS Windows, Word, Excel, Outlook, Access, Project, PowerPoint, Frontpage & Explorer skills
- Telecom Systems - Voicemail Systems, FLSMS

Training & Qualifications:

- BSc (Hons) - Geology
- 3 'A' levels
- 10 GCSE's
- MCP Windows 2000 Professional

Personal Details:

- Born 10th January, 1977
- Single
- Full clean driving licence
- References available on request

Commentary – Rob Brown

- **HEADING** – Rob's CV has been correctly headed, with his name and contact details. He has, however, only included one contact number – it is important that all contact information appears on your CV as this ensures that you are easily contactable.

- **VISUAL LAYOUT** – As in the previous example, Rob has used complex formatting. He has also used Verdana as a font – the most acceptable fonts types are Arial and Times New Roman, with a minimum font size of 10 and 11-points respectively.
- **LENGTH** – At two pages, the length of Rob's CV is just right.
- **STRUCTURE** – Rob has presented all information in the correct order and his sentences and paragraphs are a good length, making his CV quick and easy to read.
- **ENGLISH LANGUAGE** – His command of the English language is good, and there are no spelling or grammatical errors.
- **PROFILE** – His profile is well written and does a good selling job.
- **EMPLOYMENT HISTORY** – First, Rob's work history reads more little like a job description. He needs to focus more on his achievements and emphasise how his current and previous employers have benefited from his work. Where appropriate, Rob should back up these benefits with tangible facts and figures. Second, he has included no company names. Although it is not mandatory to include who you have worked for, if you do not include the company name, it is advisable to provide a brief company description at the very least.
- **ACHIEVEMENTS** – It is essential that you draw attention to your achievements as it provide employers with an insight into what you can achieve for their organisation and what the benefit of hiring you would be. Rob has purely listed facts and provided no achievements. He needs to highlight between three and five of his major achievements, focusing on those that will be particularly relevant to his target position.
- **EDUCATIONAL HISTORY** – His educational history and professional development have been expressed well.

Conclusion

Although Rob's CV has some good content, he is making a classic mistake – he is underselling himself. There needs to be more focus on his skills and achievements, and the presentation is also letting him down.

In the next two pages, you can review Rob's revised CV after it was professionally reformatted. Soon after Rob's CV was posted on the internet, he received three interviews and secured two job offers, one of which resulted in a 40% increase in salary.

REVISED CV – ROB BROWN

Rob Brown

3 No Name Close, London SW1
Tel (h): 020 1234567 Tel (m): 07123 456789
E-mail: rbrown@abcd.com

PROFESSIONAL PROFILE

A highly proficient **Senior Test Analyst,** educated to degree level, with considerable experience within the telecommunications market sector. Excellent skills in testing Universal Voice Messaging Systems and Fixed Line Short Messaging System applications. Well-developed leadership skills, with the ability to motivate in a pressurised environment. An adaptable, approachable and results-oriented individual with excellent organisational and communication skills. Enjoys working in a team environment and achieving team and personal goals.

MAJOR ACHIEVEMENTS

* Implemented test entry check sheet for XYZ's clients, to complete prior to onsite testing, providing a clear indication to the state of the environment before testing was performed, saved an average of three days testing per client
* Instigated the design for new order lines at XYZ, improving their simplicity to the public. The new functionality used fixed line test messaging, which provided higher revenues and a significant reduction in the number of complaints
* Introduced a transfer of information meeting with the operation teams to provide up-to-date information on new installs on the live servers. This improved the process by allowing operations to analyse and solve routine problems before they were escalated to support
* Produced a business plan concerning the test teams travel costs to client sites, suggesting the idea of new travel allowances, saving the company £6K per annum
* Identified key areas for training and skills within the Test Team with the objective of providing a more efficient and competitive service to the client base. Training courses and workshops were implemented, producing a highly motivated and productive team

PROFESSIONAL EXPERIENCE

ABC plc: Milton Keynes   **Sep 1999–Present**

Test Analyst   **Jan 2003–Present**

* Responsible for end-to-end management of testing for key projects, involving complex business systems and integration testing
* Successfully installing and upgrading HW and SW within agreed project timescales
* Took a pro-active approach in instigating capacity planning to produce performance metrics
* Scheduling and delivering real-time and out-of-hours support, providing excellent systems administration and quality service to users
* Managing the regular review and production of technical specifications and test documents; influential in providing comprehensive test preparation
* Prime instigator for the rebuild and new configuration of unified messaging within the test environment
* Defining and executing all test activities, including training and documentation
* Managing various stages within the test cycle, including component, system (functional and non-functional) integration and UAT testing
* Creating and executing test scripts and plans over widespread functions for clients, including full test lifecycle for customised voicemail and unified messaging systems
* Member of the out-of-hours XYZ client support group, diagnosing faults and providing rapid resolutions to customer problems
* Achieved the 'Silver Award' for outstanding commitment to client services
* Controlling the co-ordination of testing across all components for major XYZ projects
* Investigating ABC's program failures through de-bugging and developing required changes

- Mentoring junior members of staff ensuring that they have a seamless transition from junior to senior test analyst
- Co-ordinating work with specialists, solutions engineers and clients, as required
- Working with both internal and external suppliers in order to investigate, analyse and resolve test faults
- Reviewing test results and ensuring incident reports are raised as necessary
- Tracking, chasing, retesting and closing faults
- Ensured all documentation written for releases was to a QMS (Quality Management System) standard

Operations Shift Leader   **Sep 2002–Jan 2003**

- Responsible for problem and change management for ABC's Mainframes in live test environments, including all elements of comprehensive Voicemail System Service activities
- Managed a four-man shift ensuring all operational duties were carried out and maintained. Supported the shift members and set objectives ensuring targets were achievable and exceeded
- Produced and maintained general operational procedures in conjunction with service review requirements
- Set yearly objectives for operators on shift, holding quarterly, half yearly and end of year performance reviews

Shift Operator   **Sep 1999–Sep 2002**

- Planned and delivered operational support to an extensive client base, ensuring provision of timely and high quality service deliverable to over 6m users
- Reconciled and prioritised ad-hoc customer queries and faults with daily scheduling
- Performed Hardware and Software upgrades, installations and full testing of the Unisys Mainframes
- Conducted console operations and monitoring for Unisys A Series and Clearpath Systems in a 7x24x365 Data Centre environment, observing multiple machines for alerts, alarms and indicators of abnormal processing
- Developed online and batch programming, using Unisys COBOL, Enterprise Database Server (DMSII), WFL, CANDE and Transaction Server (COMS)

COMPUTER SKILLS

Proficient with Windows Office, Windows 2000Pro and Unisys A Series Basic knowledge of Unix and GPM

EDUCATION AND PROFESSIONAL DEVELOPMENT

BSc (Hons) Greenwich University: 2.2   1999

Effective communication and presentation skills
Team leadership and motivation techniques
Hardware platforms Unisys NX5600, NX4800
OS software applications, GPM, Linux, Unisys A-series
MS Windows, Word, Excel, Outlook, Access, Project, PowerPoint,
    Frontpage and Explorer
Telecom systems – Voicemail, FLSMS
MCP in Windows 2000 Pro

PERSONAL DETAILS

Driving Licence: Full and Clean
Interests: Rugby, boxing and movies

James Black – CV

5 No Name Street,
London SW1
email : jamesblack@abcd.com
Mobile: 07123 456 789

Professional Experience
Software Engineer
MDE Systems, Winchester
November 2004 - date

Achievements
Application Response Management (ARM)
Advised on and implementation of ARM layer in core business components to manage availability and performance of systems across multiple node architectures.

Role
Support of existing and new applications, development of new ones for a rapidly growing Internet Security company. I take on and support existing code trees and use code debugging and analysers to expedite this process. New applications I develop in a way so as to be easy to maintain and support for others that follow.

As a full time developer at MDE Systems, on a daily basis, I use Accurev – source code repository and adhere to internal change control protocols. I support all projects under my control through to test, validation and load test.

UNIX tools

I am conversant with and use UNIX tools as second nature within the shell – for example, Perl, Bash, sed, grep vi and am happy at the command line as this is often more productive than other interfaces can be. I administer many aspects of UNIX systems as part of my role and have working knowledge from previous positions to draw from (of upward to 10 years working with UNIX at all levels). For example the following list is a few of the tools / services that I regularly use and can administer as part of my current role:

NTP – time synchronisation between servers
DNS – IP resolution up to Bind9
FTP – configuration of servers, ACL's, scripted clients, ncftp, sftp
rsync – keeping directories synchronised across multiple hosts
NFS – mountd sharing UNIX file systems with other UNIX hosts
RPM – rpmbuild, the build of new RPM packages and installation, upgrade and audit of existing packages
SSHD – public / private key authentication using commercial and Open-SSH, SSHD setup and configuration
Samba – to share UNIX file systems with Windows
Iptables – statefull firewall used to protect systems and as Internet Gateways
PPTP – secure tunnel client (Linux and windows)
rdesktop and vnc – remote desktop administration for Windows NT and 200X from Linux
EXT2/EXT3 file systems – partitioning, re-partitioning, backup, restore and re-sizing of partitions together with database
partimaged – disk image backups and disaster recovery
Bluez – Bluetooth stack for linux t/w GPRS mobile Internet access
MDE Systems uses RedHat Linux which I have worked with for nearly 10 years and I now personally use Mandrake (Mandriva) and Gentoo linux distributions . . .

Education
I am educated to degree level and hold a Bsc (Hons) in Technology Management from ABC University, the main aim of which was to produce high quality 'hybrid' technology workers with a firm grounding in Software Development, principles of Structured Systems Analysis and Design Methodologies and the ability to manage technological change and innovation.

B.Sc.(Hons)
Technology Management 2:1
ABC University
1991-1995 inclusive 1 year sandwich placement as Trainee Programmer for BCT Security Products

BTEC HNC Computer Studies
ABC Polytechnic (Part time evening and day release)
1989-91

11 GSE 'O' Levels
XYZ School
1982-85

Courses & Training over last 3 years
Personal study and training – ongoing and constant.
YAPC (Perl) 2004, 2005 booked
Linux Professional Institute Parts I & II (personal study) - ongoing
Sun Microsystems - Solaris 9
Sun Microsystems - Veritas and Sun Cluster
Sun Microsystems - Solaris Admin Part I and II
AIX UNIX – introductory course to systems administration.

Skills
Software
Perl 5 (from 1997 some Perl 4 to present day Perl 5.8.x both from CPAN Perl and Activestate Win32)
Mysql 3.x – 5
Microsoft SQL Server 6.5,7.0, 2000
Apache web server 1.3x 2.X
Microsoft IIS 4.0

Security
For systems that I build and complete architectures I use penetration testing tools, Nessus for example, to find and analyse breaches and other short falls in security. I use Linux iptable firewalls for my own networks and set up solutions for others in my spare time. I have modified 'Smoothwall' firewall to provide content filtering and parental control system including Internet Messaging logging tools to capture and audit MSN logging information for Parental Control and supervision.

Operating Systems
I have administered and implemented the automated roll out of UNIX, for example Linux, Solaris, DEC-OSF, HP and Windows NT 4 through to 2003. I am formally trained to cluster server with Solaris and Veritas Volume Manager. I am fully conversant with the following:
UNIX
Redhat Linux 7.x, 8.0, 9, ES2.1-3.0, FC3
Mandrake 6-10.2 (2005-LE)
Gentoo
Solaris 6,7,8,9

Windows
NT4.0, 2000, 2003

Network Protocols
I have designed and implemented many network based solutions using for example, TCP/
IP, HTTP(S), UDP, SNMP protocols. This has involved developing client and server based
solutions and re-using server solutions such as mod_Perl, SOAP on Apache and IIS web
services. These have all had to be security driven and implemented on secured Internet
solutions adhering to security standards both internally set and officially accepted, e.g./
BS7799.

Personal Credibility
In order for me to work on Internet Banking solutions for example, ABD Personal Finance
(CPA Plc), and national government, including networks for government such at CDE, I was
cleared to work on Restricted and Confidential systems.

I have at all times protected the integrity and secure running of the systems under my control.
This has involved reporting internal breaches and bad practice and managing any rectification
work and updates to procedures as required.

Systems Management, Self Management, Management of Others
I have implemented and designed various networked solutions to solve an array of different
problems, such as the integration of XYZ Managed Services management systems to work
with other management systems such as CWD Ltd. I have managed the migration of the core
business infrastructure to a distributed solution in a major project taking upwards of a year
to complete. This meant the migrating of all customers to use new Internet Managed core
services which I also implemented such as DNS, Email, FTP, Monitoring, NTP, and Trusted
Host access and management systems. This was a major technical and physical undertaking
for which I took personal responsibility for as a Technical Design Authority. Together with
management of the migration, I actually did an large amount of the hands on work as is
the style of doing things in fast moving commercial Internet businesses. This involved also
managing others to get changes on all customers that used the infrastructure. There was no
business failure or loss of service and no customers were lost.

Programming Design and Implementation Methods
For anything from a small project to a large one, I apply the following approach.

Software is documented from the start and included in the code as it is written. The interface
is designed and documented prior to coding.

I also employ entity relationship modelling, structured English and database normalisation

I regularly give presentations. As part of my role over the last six years this has been an
integral part of project working. These have been both formal and informal, the latter, where no
preparation or planning is possible and in front of both peers and managers.

Outside work I give presentations for technical programming groups that meet in Birmingham
and elsewhere.

Commentary – James Black

Before commenting on this CV it is important to note that this CV was originally four pages long and written in a 7-point font size. Large portions of the CV have been removed and the font size has been increased for the purposes of this book.

- **HEADING** – James' CV has been correctly headed with his name and contact details; he does, however need to enlarge his name to make it more of a focal point. He has also included a title, i.e. the word 'CV'; the appearance of a title or a heading is unnecessary, as it should be obvious what the document is.

- **VISUAL LAYOUT** – The general layout of his CV needs to be dramatically improved as it is not reader-friendly or appealing to the eye. At 7-points, the font size was far too small; this needs to increased to a minimum of 10-points.

- **LENGTH** – James' CV, at four pages was far too long and needs to be cut down to no more than three pages; ideally two.

- **STRUCTURE** – James' CV does not constitute an accepted CV structure as first, it is difficult to follow because of the way the information has been presented and second, no bullet points have been used. The use of bullet points is important as this will makes a CV easy to read and punchy.

- **ENGLISH LANGUAGE** – There is one grammatical error and a spelling mistake, which creates a very bad first impression. CVs must be checked and double-checked for these types of errors.

- **PROFILE** – James has not included a profile. As mentioned in previous examples, a CV is a sales document and including a profile provides an opportunity to sell your skills, experience and achievements.

- **KEY SKILLS** – Importantly, James has mentioned his skills, both technical and other, but the problem is, he mentions them on the last page of his CV. Not only are they very long-winded but being on page four, it is unlikely the reader will last until then. His skills need to be mentioned on the first page of his CV. They should be tweaked and re-ordered depending on the role being applied for, i.e. the most important/relevant ones should be listed first.

- **EMPLOYMENT HISTORY** – His current role has been poorly presented and does not provide enough information. There is too much focus on the tools he is using and not enough on what he achieved with each of those tools. In his role at XYZ Managed Services, there is too much focus on responsibilities and not enough on achievements. James needs to place more emphasis on how his employers have benefited from his work and where appropriate, he needs to quantify his achievements.

- **ACHIEVEMENTS** – Although James mentions his achievements, these are lost as the information has been so poorly presented. He needs to shout about his achievements and it is recommended that he has a separate section where he can highlight three to five of his major achievements, ideally those within the last five years and those that will be most relevant to his target position.

- **EDUCATIONAL HISTORY** – His educational history and professional development have been expressed well, but as he has a degree and over two years' work experience, he need not provide details of how many GSEs he achieved.

Conclusion

This is a good example of a CV that is likely to get binned purely because the presentation is letting it down. James has excellent skills, experience and achievements but this is all lost due to the poor presentation of the information.

If you continue to the next page, you will see a well-presented nicely laid out CV, which resulted in James receiving an interview, and thereafter a job offer, from the first company he sent it to.

REVISED CV – JAMES BLACK

James Black

5 No Name Street, London SW1
Tel (m): 07123456 789
Email: jamesblack@abcd.com

PROFESSIONAL PROFILE

An innovative Software Engineer and Solutions Designer, with a proven track record of success with experience of both public and private sector contracts. Consistent development and utilisation of specialist skills within Component Level applications, writing and designing user interfaces with object-oriented development.

A determined, organised technical strategic analyst with a performance record in both problem solving and delivery. Results orientated and quality-focused with project planning skills.

Key strength areas include: developing and delivering effective software solutions, analysis and design functions, with a broad knowledge of development tools. Proven ability for incorporating testing, planning and implementation activities with efficiency and reliability initiatives.

AREAS OF EXPERTISE

- Managed Services
- SQL Disaster Recovery
- Restricted Networks
- Technical Design and Management
- Application Programming and Testing
- System Security
- Systems Design, Support and Build
- Systems Administration

KEY SKILLS

- Incorporating best practice into all systems for compliance with BS7799
- Providing timely and high-quality applications that meet specifications
- Fully conversant with full development lifecycle and system analysis documentation
- Knowledge of principal platforms and hardware
- Good troubleshooting ability with remedial solution design
- Solid customer communication and interpersonal relationship skills
- Developing balance with IT requirement and business needs
- Well-defined planning, co-ordination and organisational skills

CAREER HIGHLIGHTS

- Implemented Disaster Recovery systems and Rapid System Deployment, with successful design and implementation of database replication and backup systems.
- Provided consultancy for web-based management solutions to maintain security of IP and host address information for banks and other e-commerce businesses.
- Migrated an entire infrastructure from a major ABD/XYZ site to three data centres; successfully implemented with zero downtime or loss of business.

PROFESSIONAL EXPERIENCE

MDE Systems, Winchester   **2004 to Date**

Software Engineer

- Appointed to manage key development projects and to provide training and support to junior programmers.
- Responsible for verifying and resolving complex programming issues, correcting coding mistakes to deliver stable and reliable applications
- Constructed a high profile application to control and manage the network flow of email, identifying and blocking potential SPAM emails.
- Developed a program for movement and management of log files.
- Provide technical project management, team development and mentoring to ensure timely delivery of key projects.

XYZ Managed Services, Cheshire   **1998 to 2004**

Senior Engineer

- Designed and implemented many key client applications and in-house systems, many of which are still utilised with few enhancements.

173

- Implemented secure 'trusted host' access for remote access to secure systems using SSH and public/private key authentication.
- Completed disaster recovery and business continuity planning and testing for major business critical databases, with regular testing and subsequent reviews.
- Designed, developed and implemented new infrastructure to handle technology advancement.
- Development Examples:
XYZ IMS Wintel Service monitoring tool
Outpost a website monitoring tool for performance and availability
SystemManager equivalent of CND Ltd, TWA OpenView and JKL
Integrated SystemManager with CND Ltd and XYZ SiteChecker
- Client portfolio included: ABD Personal Finance, CPA Plc and Government Networks.

FPC Limited, Cheshire   **1998**

Computer Support Analyst (9-month contract)

- Responsible for the verification of an in-house Y2K compliance audit.
- Completed end user support for 130 desktop and PC users.
- Developed and implemented a web based graphical gateway to CAD/CAM systems.

EARLY CAREER

Software Technician, ABC University	**1996 to 1998**
Voluntary and Contract Work for DEC	**1995 to 1996**
Trainee Programmer, BCT Security Products (sandwich placement)	**1995**
Engineer, Office Clerk, Data Preparation	**1985 to 1991**

COMPUTER SKILLS

- **Software:** Perl – from CPAN Perl and Activestate Win32, Mysql, Microsoft SQL Server, Apache web server, Microsoft IIS 4.0
- **Security:** Penetration Test Tools, Nessus, Iptable Firewall, Smoothwall, PGP and GPG public/private key encryption
- **Operating Systems:** Linux, Solaris, DEC-OSF, Cluster Server, UNIX, Redhat Linux 7.x, 8.0, 9, ES2.1-3.0, FC3, Mandrake 6-10.2 (2005-LE), Gentoo, Solaris 6,7,8,9, Windows, NT4.0, 2000, 2003
- **Network Protocols:** TCP/IP, HTTP(S), UDP, SNMP, mod_Perl, SOAP
- **Systems Management:** Fujitsu Internet, CA Unicenter, Infrastructure Migration, Distributed Solutions, DNS, Email, FTP, Monitoring, NTP, Trusted Host Access

EDUCATION AND PROFESSIONAL DEVELOPMENT

BSc (Hons) Technology Management, ABC University	1995
BTEC HNC Computer Studies	1991

YAPC (Perl) 2004
PHP (personal study) – ongoing
Javascript (personal study) – ongoing
Linux Professional Institute Parts I & II (personal study) – ongoing
Sun Microsystems – Solaris 9, Veritas and Sun Cluster, Solaris Admin Part I and II
AIX UNIX – introductory course to systems administration

PERSONAL DETAILS

Driving Licence:	Full, UK driving licence
Security clearance:	Cleared to work on Restricted and Confidential Government Systems
Location:	Willing to travel
Interests:	Property renovation, cooking, cycling and hill walking, technology and programming projects – created a content filter, secure proxy and parental control system for home use using Smoothwall, SquidGuard and custom Perl modules to monitor MSN conversations.

ORIGINAL CV – PONCHO DEVAGA

Flat 2
No Name Street
Greenwich
London

SE10

Date of Birth 02/07/1975
Nationality   USA
Permanent Resident
Email   poncho.devaga@abcd.com

Poncho Devaga

Education

Grand Valley State University (Grand Rapids MI)   1995-1999
Bachelor of Science in Commuincations
* Public Relations
* Advertising
* Business(minor)

Kingston University
University Exchange Program- Business School   Oct 1996- June 1997

Employment History

KXG Limited   Feb 04- Present
Membership Sales Consultant
Duty Manager

Responsiblities

- To sell both individual and corporate membership packages.
- Maintian existing corporate member accounts.
- Maintian and regulate all aspects of club operations and standards.
- Maintain and develop sound relationships with club members and stafff

XYZ Leisure Consultancy   July 03- Dec 03
Membership Sales Consultant

Responsibilities

- Increasing membership sales at two 5 star London hotel leisure clubs; ABC Garden Court, CFG Hotels
- Researching and identifying local businesses to establish corporate membership busisness.

SYZ Robotics   Jan 02-Mar 03
Marketing/PR Executive

A small engineering company recently established specializing in integration systems for measurement, inspection, calibration and postioning of 3D objects. Specifically directed to the provision of jigs and fixtures for military aircraft.

Responsibilities

- To design and construct a preleiminary marketing plan and layout overall marketing strategies to provide SYZ Systems with a platform for maximum exposure and penetration into the aero-manufacturing market.

- To conduct market research and anaylsis of potential customers and assessment of global OEM production requirements.

- To create maximum awareness of SYZ system demostration through various mediums
  Trade Shows
  Press Release

TGF Health Club   2000-2001
Membership Consultant

Responsibilities

- To sell individual and corporate memberships
- Working in conjuntion and liasing with varios health and beauty companies to set up integrated product promotions.

ACC Publications Limited (London) *
International Media Sales Executive

XAZ Defence - an international trade publication, which analyses the latest developments in military technology in sea, air, and land systems. Specifically desgined to aid ministries of defence in their procurement of military goods.

Responsibilities

- To sell advertising space to aero-defence companies.
- Attending trade shows and exhibitions to liase with government officials and various military organizations to establish perceptions on government needs towards defence procurement.

Other Interest
Golf
Fishing
Running

Commentary – Poncho Devega

Before commenting on Poncho's CV, it is important to note that the font size was originally 9-points; we have increased the font size for the purpose of this book.

- **HEADING** – Although Poncho's CV has been correctly headed with his name and contact details, it is recommended that your name appear before your address details. If your address appears first, this can cause some scanners difficulties and you may find that your name changes from 'Poncho Devaga' to 'Flat 2', in which case, you will lose out on any potential vacancies that may arise. It is also vital that you include ALL contact information on your CV, as this allows for you to be contacted easily. Poncho has only provided his email address, which is restrictive.
- **VISUAL LAYOUT** – Poncho has ensured that there is a lot of white space in his CV, which makes his CV easy on the eye but the gaps are too large and are not consistent.
- **LENGTH** – At two pages, the length of his CV is just right but due to the large gaps of white space, it is almost looks as though he is trying to fill up the two pages by using a lot of white space.
- **STRUCTURE** – The overall structure of Poncho's CV is good; sentences and paragraphs are a good length. Information has, however, not been presented in the correct order, for example, as he has over two years' work experience, his educational history needs to appear at the end of his CV.
- **ENGLISH LANGUAGE** – Poncho's CV is awash with spelling mistakes. It shows a lack of attention to detail and will provide a very bad impression. Despite the fact he is a good candidate with great skills, the likelihood is that his CV will be binned after the second spelling mistake is spotted or in some cases, the first.
- **PROFILE** – Poncho, as with many potential candidates, has failed to include a profile. As mentioned previously this is a great opportunity to sell yourself and as your CV is your sales tool, it is vital to include.
- **OBJECTIVE** – Poncho has not included a career objective. Poncho has had a varied career and has worked across a broad range of industries; an objective will help provide focus to his CV. He needs to keep it specific, but not constrictive and he needs to describe what kind of job he is seeking and what he can contribute to the company in return.
- **KEY SKILLS** – Poncho should include a section entitled 'Key Skills' or 'Areas of Expertise' where he can summarise his skills and responsibilities

in relation to his target position. If you have no direct experience, this is a great opportunity to outline your transferable skills.

- **EMPLOYMENT HISTORY** – It is very common mistake to produce a job description as Poncho has done here. Instead, Poncho needs to emphasise how his employers have benefited from his work. Where appropriate, he needs to quantify these benefits by providing tangible facts and figures. The type of thing he can include here are any special skills or knowledge he possesses or has acquired that will allow him to perform tasks satisfactorily; where he has made or saved money for the company; any initiatives he has introduced; comments made by peers or managers.

- **ACHIEVEMENTS** – People find it difficult to sell themselves and as such, very often do not include a section detailing their career highlights or key achievements. Poncho needs to include a separate section where he can highlight three or four of his major achievements. He must include details of the task, his involvement/actions and the result or business benefit thereof.

- **EDUCATIONAL HISTORY** – This section has been expressed well but needs to appear at the end of his CV as his practical experience outweighs his degree and qualifications.

- **COMPUTER SKILLS** – Poncho has provided no mention of his IT skills. In this day and age, it is essential that you are computer literate and consequently, it is important to detail your proficiency with various packages and systems.

Conclusion

This CV is a classic example of someone who is underselling themselves. Poncho has provided very little information on his CV and certainly has not provided a prospective employer with any idea of what he is capable of. The presentation is also letting him down as the font size is not consistent and there are large gaps of white space throughout. The biggest mistake that he has made, however, is not checking his CV for spelling mistakes or grammatical errors. This is an immediate turn-off to a prospective employer as it not only shows a lack of attention-to-detail but it creates a poor impression of the individual.

After Poncho had his CV professionally reformatted, he received multiple responses from several companies and within one month, he went on to secure the job that he was looking for. His revised CV can be viewed in the next two pages.

REVISED CV – PONCHO DEVAGA

Poncho Devaga

Flat 2 No Name Street, Greenwich, London, SE1
Tel (h): 0123 456 789 Tel (m): 07123 456 789
Email: poncho.devaga@abcd.com

OBJECTIVE

Seeking to secure a challenging position in the aerospace industry, utilising both academic success and commercial experience gained in the areas of direct sales, PR and advertising.

PROFESSIONAL PROFILE

A career driven and confident **Sales professional**, with experience across a variety of industries including leisure, advertising and engineering sales. Developed a strong performance record of consistently achieving sales targets and producing an immediate bottom-line impact. Experienced at implementing strategy in both sales and marketing environments.

Results and profit-focused, with excellent relationship management skills. Recognised as determined, ambitious, energetic and out-going with high levels of versatility, enthusiasm and drive.

Key strength areas include: initiation and sustenance of new business opportunities, customer focus, achieving set sales targets, delivering under pressure and managing internal and external business contacts.

KEY SKILLS

- Adept at concept selling for new product launch and new technology
- Flexible communication style – adapting to audience including senior management
- Negotiation and influencing
- Account and Customer Relationship Management (CRM)
- Sales and Business Development strategies
- Adaptable within working environment, supporting all areas of business as required

CAREER HIGHLIGHTS

- Consistently met sales targets, targeting customers on both a cold-call basis and referral sales.
- Achieved a sales conversion rate of 40–45% with management commendation for success.
- Established a good ability to seek and identify new clients, both on an individual and corporate basis.

PROFESSIONAL EXPERIENCE

KXG Limited, Chelsea   **2004 to Date**

Membership Consultant/Duty Manager
- Responsible for membership sales, targeting individual and corporate membership at a very high profile gym with celebrity membership.
- Completion of Duty Manager role ensuring club standards for customer service, health and safety, and operational standards are maintained.
- Provision of leadership and guidance for staff members with 1-2-1 sales coaching.
- Establish customer requirements, taking pride in personally understanding customer needs and ensuring appropriate solutions offered.
- Set-up corporate membership, dealing with HR departments selling benefit of employee fitness; negotiating special rates and providing input for corporate websites.

XYZ Leisure Consultancy, London   **Mar to Dec 2003**

Membership Sales Consultant
- Responsible for increasing club membership sales and promoted customer retention through high standards of customer service.

- Completed direct mailing exercises with follow up calls; successful at converting initial calls into appointments and demonstrating club facilities.
- Increased membership sales at two five-star London hotel leisure clubs: ABC Garden Court and CFG Hotels.
- Researched and identified local business to establish corporate membership business.
- Completed reception, customer service and administration duties as required.

SYZ Robotics, London   **2002 to 2003**
Aerospace Engineering

Marketing/PR Executive
- Responsible within a start-up organisation for development of sales and marketing strategies for new product and new market launch. Introduced specialist equipment for the provision of jigs and fixtures for military aircraft.
- Identified target market and completed competitor analysis to form effective plans for the product launch, including PR communications and media planning.
- Created optimum awareness of new product and business ability through a variety of mediums including trade shows and press releases.
- Completed detailed analysis to establish global OEM production requirements.

TFG Health Club, London   **2000 to 2001**
Membership Consultant
- Responsible for pre-sales activities for a new health club. Joined three months prior to opening, to achieve club membership for launch date.
- Developed highly tuned concept sales skills, achieving good results in attainment of corporate membership.
- Completed campaigns of direct sales, both cold calling and following existing leads.
- Following club opening, continued to increase membership sales with high conversion rates for walk-in clients.

ACC Publications Limited, London   **1999 to 2000**
Trade Publication Firm

International Media Sales Executive
- Responsible for selling advertising space for XAZ Defence, an international trade publication within the defence industry.
- Completed cold calling campaigns, targeting large international aerospace organisations.
- Skilled at identifying key personnel and decision makers and converting leads into sales.
- Attended trade shows and exhibitions; liased with government officials and various military organisations to establish government's needs towards defence procurement.

COMPUTER SKILLS

Proficient user of Microsoft Word, Excel, PowerPoint; competent Touch Typist

EDUCATION AND PROFESSIONAL DEVELOPMENT

BSc communications PR/ADV: Grand Valley State University   1999
Modules: Public Relations, Advertising and Business Studies

ADDITIONAL DETAILS

Nationality: American with Permanent UK Residency
Location: Willing to travel or relocate
Interests: Golfing, Fishing, Weight Training and Running

CURRICULUM VITAE

PERSONAL DETAILS:

NAME: *Alan Jones*
ADDRESS: *18 Peacock Street, London SE2*
TELEPHONE: *0123 456 789*   **MOBILE:** *07123456 789*
E-MAIL: *alan.jones@abcd.net*
DATE OF BIRTH: *15th August 1967*
STATUS: *Married*

PROFESSIONAL PROFILE:

"An experienced yet adaptable production & operations led business manager with a proven track record of success within a variety of highly competitive environments."

"Strong all-round leadership experience within a wide portfolio of commercial sectors."

"A results orientated professional with excellent communication, negotiation, and business planning skills."

"Broad experience of the deployment of major production initiatives, now looking to further develop towards a senior business management role where rewards match results."

CAREER TO DATE:

2004 to date:
OPERATIONS MANAGER   (Reports to the Managing Director)
ABC Limited – *London*
Manufacturer / fabricator of kitchen and bathroom work surfaces

* Leadership of a multi-site operation - 3 units RED, 1 unit BLU. *P&L responsibility*
* Key customers include; MCA Plc, XYZ Plc, WBA Limited
* Providing solutions for DIY retail, OEM's, merchants and general distributors

Key achievements include:
* Set the Company on a lean manufacturing change programme, involving every employee
* Successfully coached 130 employees through NVQ II in Business Process Improvement Techniques
* Established key performance indicators and company wide process control
* Dramatically improved IFOTIS (in full, on time, in spec)

2003 to 2004:
PRODUCTION MANAGER   (Reported to the Managing Director)
JDD Limited – *Lancashire.*
Manufacturer of domestic soft furnishings

* Responsible for the day-to-day management of the production facility, 200 employees. *P & L responsibility*
* Managed an extensive PBR system
* Key customers included; IQT Plc, XYZ Plc, WBA Limited

Key achievements include:
* Lead a major cost down programme in partnership with IQT plc
* Carried out a detailed people and process assessment resulting in a fundamental restructure
* Increased throughput by circa 25%. Contributed towards a substantial profit increase

2002 to 2003:
GROUP OPERATIONS MANAGER   (Reported to the Group Operations Director)
LJP Furniture Group PLC – *Essex*
Supplier / installer of office furniture systems

* Responsible for operations across two sites: - Essex and Edinburgh
* Ensures value-based operations across all sites.
* Key customers include; CDA Plc, STP Limited, UVO Plc

Key achievements include:
* Successful involvement in the development of strategic alliances within the Scottish operation
* Development of a "stand alone" business unit for the Edinburgh operation

cont:-

1998 to 2002:
WORKS MANAGER / OPERATIONS MANAGER   (Reported to the Managing Director)
PQR Furniture PLC – *Derbyshire*
Manufacturer / installer of office furniture systems

* Leadership of an extensive operations team including Manufacturing, Production Planning & Control
  Purchasing, Warehouse & Distribution, Installation, Quality, Health and Safety 300+ staff
* Ensures application of "World Class" and "Lean manufacturing" tools & techniques
* Handles budgets, forecasts & schedules

Key achievements include:
* Cycle time order to delivery, reduced by 50%. Introduced key documents to track performance
* Improved Delivery Schedule Achievement (DSA) to over 95%
* Reorganised production areas improving Floor Space Utilisation (FSU) by 30%

1996 to 1998:
PRODUCTION PLANNING & CONTROL MANAGER   (Reported to the Operations Director)
PQR Furniture PLC – *Derbyshire*

* Responsible for £30 million production planning activities
* Management of production teams – Wood processing, Assembly, Metal processing and finishing operation
* Handled budgets, forecasts & schedules

Key achievements include:
* Improved Stock Turns (ST) by 25%
* Increased throughput using *OPT* and *TOC* techniques
* Implemented capacity planning and finite scheduling systems

1994 to 1996:
TEAM LEADER - CONTINUOUS IMPROVEMENT   (Reported to the Operations Director)
PQR Furniture PLC – *Derbyshire*
* Senior production management role
* Leadership of a multi-functional team of staff, including Maintenance, Production and Product Engineering
* Introduced new production layouts following the "lean" philosophy

Key achievements include:
* Dramatically improved people productivity using value analysis techniques
* Successfully introduced *Kaizen* tools and techniques

EARLY CAREER INCLUDES:
* *Assembly Superintendent - PQR Furniture PLC*
* *Team Leader - PQR Furniture PLC*
* *Production Planner – CDE Furniture Ltd*
* *Storekeeper – CDE Furniture Ltd*
* *Weapons Engineering Mechanic - HM Royal Navy*
* *General Assistant - NBB Furniture Limited*

EDUCATION & PROFESSIONAL TRAINING:
* MSc in Manufacturing Management & Technology (Open University)
* Postgraduate Diploma in Manufacturing (Open University)
* NEBS Diploma in Management (University of Derby)
* Certificate in International Operations Management (Open University)
* Certificate in Quality: Delivering Excellence (Open University)
* Certificate in Integrated Safety, Health and Environmental Management (Open University)
* Certificate in Structure & Design of Manufacturing Systems (Open University)
* NEBS Certificate in Supervisory Management (University of Derby)
* 'O' level qualifications in six subjects
* Various in-house & external training programmes

ADDITIONAL INFORMATION:
* Wide interest in Lean Manufacturing   * Excellent PC and IT skills
* Worked within a variety of Quality and Environmental systems   * Excellent health & safety record
* Extensive knowledge of ERP, MRP and APS systems   * Clean full driving licence
* Interests include football, fitness, music & mountain-biking

* Excellent references available upon request   Alan Jones

182

Commentary – Alan Jones

Before commenting on this CV it is worth noting that some of Alan's CV information has been removed for the purpose of this book.

- **HEADING** – Alan has included the words 'Curriculum Vitae', which is not necessary as it should be clear what the document is. His CV ought to be headed with just his name and contact details.
- **VISUAL LAYOUT** – The general layout appears a little cramped and Alan's font size varies from section to section. A better use of white space is necessary and his font size should be consistent.
- **LENGTH** – At two pages, the length of his CV is perfect.
- **STRUCTURE** – The overall structure of Alan's CV is good. Sentences and paragraphs are a good length, and all information has been presented in the correct order.
- **ENGLISH LANGUAGE** – His use of the English language is good, and there are no obvious spelling or grammatical errors.
- **PROFILE** – Alan's profile does a good selling job and is well written as he has adequately summarised his core area of expertise, his skills, strengths and aspirations.
- **KEY SKILLS** – Alan has not included a key skills section and this would be to his detriment. A key skills section would allow him to quickly summarise his skills and responsibilities.
- **EMPLOYMENT HISTORY** – Alan's work history has been well presented and importantly, he has provided detail of his achievements in each of his roles. He has not expressed his actions and in some instances has not quantified or explained the business benefit of his actions.
- **ACHIEVEMENTS** – Alan's CV is achievement focused but unless he has a dedicated achievement section, some of these could be lost.
- **EDUCATIONAL HISTORY** – His educational history has been expressed well.

Conclusion

Overall, Alan's CV has some good content. He has introduced himself well in the professional profile and he has focused on what he has achieved for each of his employers. This is a great example of a good CV that has been badly presented.

In the subsequent two pages you are able to review the CV that went on to secure Alan a substantial new position with a major corporate business.

Alan Jones MSc

18 Peacock Street, London SE2
Tel (h): 0123 456 789 Tel (m): 07123 456 789
Email: alan.jones@abcd.net

PROFESSIONAL PROFILE

A committed, focused and highly professional **Senior Manager** with extensive experience in operations, manufacturing and in the deployment of major production initiatives. Possesses strong all-round leadership capabilities across a variety of commercial sectors and a proven track record of success within highly competitive environments. Results-oriented with excellent communication, negotiation, and business planning skills. Recognised as self-motivated and positive with an innate ability to remain calm under pressure.

AREAS OF EXPERTISE

• Lean Manufacturing Implementation • Developing Teams • Production Planning & Control
• Process/Manufacturing Control Techniques • Customer Focus • Change Management
• Supply Chain Management • Business Integration • P&L Responsibility

KEY SKILLS

- Leading extensive operational teams of up to 300 staff across multiple sites and disciplines including Manufacturing, Production Planning & Control Purchasing, Warehouse & Distribution, Installation, Quality, and Health & Safety
- Ensuring value-based operations across all sites and the application of 'World Class' and 'Lean manufacturing' tools and techniques
- Extensive knowledge of ERP, MRP and APS systems
- Working within a variety of Quality and Environmental systems
- Account managing key customers including MCA Plc, XYZ plc, WBA Ltd and IQT plc
- Controlling budgets, forecasts and schedules of up to £20m

RECENT CAREER HIGHLIGHTS

- Implemented a lean manufacturing change programme at ABC Limited (ABC) and educated 130 employees through NVQ II in 'Business Process Improvement Techniques'. This resulted in a significant improvement in service levels, typically 90% first time delivery, and enabled staff to focus collectively on business objectives
- Restructured the operational structure at ABC, including the management team, saving circa £300k. Resulted in a 'Team Leader' and value-added based approach
- Reorganised cutting and edging machining section at ABC, changing layout into a 'U' shape continuous flow arrangement, which increased production capacity by 25%
- Set-up a resource and capacity planning model at ABC for main production lines; resulted in 'people productivity' increases of 20%
- Restructured the management team at JDD Limited and sourced raw materials from Asia, which realised cost savings of £50k
- Made a significant contribution to breaking profit target of £1m for the first time at JDD

PROFESSIONAL EXPERIENCE

ABC LTD: London   **2004–Date**
Operations Manager

- Manage a team of 130 staff through nine direct reports, reporting to the MD, and lead a multi-site operation consisting of three RED units and one BLU unit
- Account manage customer relationships of key accounts including MCA plc, XYZ plc and WBA Ltd, which accounts for £26m of the company's annual turnover
- Provide product and service solutions for DIY retail, OEMs, merchants and general distributors
- Dramatically improved IFOTIS (In Full, On-time, In-spec) from 60% to 95%
- Established KPIs and company wide process control

JDD LIMITED: Lancashire   2003–2004
Production Manager

- Supervised the day-to-day operations of the production facility consisting of 250 employees and eight direct reports, with full P&L responsibility for a business turnover of £20m
- Managed an extensive PBR (Payments By Result) system, which involved constant review and retiming exercises, recalculation of the scheme, maintenance and control
- Account managed key accounts including IQT plc, XYZ plc and WBA Ltd; IQT alone contributed to 80% of company turnover
- Led a major cost reduction programme in partnership with IQT, project managing a series of Kaizen Blitz events throughout the company. Saved JDD circa £250k and increased throughput by around 25%, resulting in a substantial increase in profits

LJP FURNITURE GROUP PLC: Essex   2002–2003
Group Operations Manager

- Oversaw day-to-day activities of this virtual operation across two sites, and account managed key customers including the CDA Plc, STP Limited and UVO Plc
- Successfully developed strategic alliances within the Scottish operation, establishing them as the sole provider of furniture and other services to the Scottish Executive
- Developed a 'stand alone' business unit for the Edinburgh operation, from developing the feasibility study through to presenting the viability of the project to the Board

PQR FURNITURE PLC: Derbyshire   1992–2002
Works Manager/Operations Manager   *1998–2002*

- Led an extensive operations team of 300+ staff across several disciplines
- Focused on delivering the production plan, which improved Delivery Schedule Achievement (DSA) from around 75% to over 95%
- Introduced key documents to track performance, which reduced order-to-delivery cycle times by 50%
- Reorganised production areas, which improved Floor Space Utilisation (FSU) by 30%

Production Planning & Control Manager   *1996–1998*

- Ran production planning activities for a £30m business and managed a small production team
- Reduced order-to-delivery cycle times, which reduced inventory levels and improved stock turns by 25%
- Increased throughput using OPT and TOC techniques, eliminating bottle necks, improving resource allocation, and reducing overtime and operating costs
- Implemented capacity planning and finite scheduling systems, which improved labour utilisation and customer satisfaction levels

Team Leader & Assembly Superintendent   *1992–1996*

EARLY CAREER

CDE Furniture Ltd: *Production Planner & Storekeeper*   1985–1992
HM Royal Navy: *Weapons Engineering Mechanic*   1984–1985
NBB Furniture Limited: *General Assistant*   1984

COMPUTER SKILLS

- Highly proficient in Microsoft Office – Word, Excel, PowerPoint and Outlook
- Extensive knowledge of using and implementing MRP and ERP based systems including, EFACS and Sage

EDUCATION AND PROFESSIONAL DEVELOPMENT

MSc in Manufacturing Management: Open University   2000

Postgraduate Diploma in Manufacturing: Open University

NEBS Diploma in Management: University of Derby

Certificate in International Operations Management: Open University

Certificate in Quality – Delivering Excellence: Open University

Certificate in Integrated Safety, Health and Environmental Management: Open University

Certificate in Structure & Design of Manufacturing Systems: Open University

NEBS Certificate in Supervisory Management: University of Derby

6 'O' levels

ORIGINAL CV – JESS GRAHAM

PERSONAL DETAILS

Address: P. O. Box 850   Email: jgraham@abcd.com
                  Dansoman   Tel: 021 123 456
                  Accra   Mobile: 0244 123 456
                                       Date of Birth: 1st December, 1978

EDUCATION

Sept. 2006 – Dec. 2006:   **Hackney Community College, London, UK**
Certificate in Corporate Banking and Financial Investment
I took this exam to show that I have a serious interest in the financial sector
The securities institute requires this exam for all professionals in the sector.

Jan 2006 – June 2006:   **London Bridge Business College, London**
Post Graduate Level – Chartered Institute of Marketing (CIM)

Sept 2002 – Dec. 2004:   **Institute of Professional Studies, Ghana**
Certificate or Advance Level, Chartered Institute of Marketing (CIM)

Sept. 1998 – Dec 2001:   **Kumasi Polytechnic, Ghana**
HND Marketing, 2nd Class Upper

Sept. 1995 – Dec. 1997:   **St. Roses' Secondary School, Ghana**
SSCE (8 subjects including English and Mathematics)

WORK EXPERIENCE

October 2005 – Jan. 2007:   **ABC Retail Shop, London, UK**
- Cash Office Administrator
- Close and open sessions
- Issue floats
- Safe spot cluck procedures
- Morning report printing
- Cashing up and finalising tills
- Investigating discrepancies
- Recording income and expense
- Reconciling extra floats
- Banking procedures
- Completing financial reports
- Change orders
- Miscellaneous cash procedures
- Accept and return vouchers to and from Head office
- Store funds safe procedures

| Jan. 2004 – May 2004: | BSA Bank, Accra – Ghana
Assistant Customer Care Officer |

- Deal with customer complaints on telephone and respond to emails and letters
- Assess customer complaints in different categories in the form if data and reports and finding solutions to them
- Assessing staff work in terms of sales target, team work, customer care and making recommendations for various awards
- Assisting service and recognition manager in administrative duties

| Jan. 2000 – March 2003: | BSA, Accra – Ghana
Front Line Staff |

- Issue bankers drafts and payment, pension and sundry payments
- Liaise with other departments to solve customer problems
- Change rates on returned cheques and post them to respective customers
- Handle overseas money transfers to customers
- Learn cashiering from tellers
- Record salaries of different companies each month

| Sept. 1999 – January 1999: | ABD Union Assurance
Assistant to Marketing Officer |

- Deal with customer enquiries via telephone and on face to face basis
- Presentation of written reports on new customer …and after sales …
- Prospecting to win new customers, visit to maintain customers and maintain mutual relationship between company and its clients

SKILLS, EXPERIENCE AND ACCOMPLISHMENTS

A talent for improving on face to face, writing, email and over the telephone
Competent team worker as a result of my work experience and the position of responsibility I held at school. I really enjoy working with diverse group of people.
Methodical in ensuring transactions are accurate
Ability to work under pressure
Adapt to plan and organise my work efficiently to ensure the smooth running of any business
Decrease costs through ensuring quality customer service
Completed a significant project in my dissertation 'Achieving Quality Customer Care Through Staff. (A case study of BSA Bank, Ghana – Prempeh II Street, Kumasi).

Through my organisation, I was able to acquire and analyse also the necessary information and complete the project on time.

OTHER SKILLS

IT Skills: Proficient in Microsoft Excel, Word, Microsoft Office 2000, Windows 95/98, Retail Java.

OTHER DATA

Enjoy sports and charity work. Contributed monies into helping the needy in my society. Enjoy meeting people and committed to my relationships, they family, work on social.

REFERENCE

References Available on Request

Commentary – Jess Graham

- **HEADING** – Jess has failed to include her name on her CV, which should really be the focal point on a CV. Although she has included her email address, it is not clear from this what her name might be. This will make it awkward for people wishing to make contact with her both via telephone or email.

- **VISUAL LAYOUT** – Although there is a lot of white space in this document, the general layout could be improved. The use of white space should be evenly spread; in Jess' CV, there are blocks of white space.

- **LENGTH** – Jess has taken her CV to just over two pages. With good formatting, two pages can easily be achieved.

- **STRUCTURE** – Jess' sentence length is too short and as such her CV is rather short on content. Additionally, education has been presented before employment history which is not correct as she has more than two years' work experience.

- **ENGLISH LANGUAGE** – Her use of the English language is good, and there are no obvious spelling or grammatical errors. She has used 'I' and 'my' throughout her CV and although this is acceptable, it is best to omit 'I' and 'my' from your CV.

- **PROFILE** – Like many of the CVs provided in this chapter, Jess has not included a profile. Jess needs to provide a summary of her skills, experience and qualifications in relation to her target position as a marketeer.

- **OBJECTIVE** – From reviewing her original CV, it is not obvious as to what her career aspirations are and as such she really needs to include an 'Objective'. She should clarify what kind of job she is looking for and what she feels she can contribute to the company.

- **KEY SKILLS** – Jess has not included a 'Key Skills' section. As she is looking to draw on previous experience, she must highlight skills from her past career and emphasise transferable skills gained from her most recent roles.

- **EMPLOYMENT HISTORY** – This is a perfect example of how to list a job description and as such, is a perfect example of how not to express your work history. Jess needs to expand on each of these points and provide detail of what her involvement has been in each of these tasks and what her accomplishments have been.

- **ACHIEVEMENTS** – As she has had a very diverse career, it may not be possible to provide relevant achievements. Jess should try to identify achievements that may be relevant to her target position but if she is unable to do so, this section can be omitted altogether.

- **EDUCATIONAL HISTORY** – Educational history has been expressed well but should be placed at the end of her CV as her practical experience outweighs her schooling and qualifications. As her marketing qualifications are important to her target position, these should be highlighted in her profile.

Conclusion

Jess' CV is a typical example of the CVs recruitment professionals see everyday. Her CV lacks direction, provides no legacy and does very little to inspire the reader. Her CV is in desperate need of a profile, an objective and a key skills section. As can be seen she provides the 'classic' job description under each of her roles.

Jess opted to have her CV professionally reformatted, which appears on the next two pages, and went on to secure five interviews. She was offered and accepted a role with a blue-chip financial services organisation.

Jess Graham

P.O Box 850, Dansoman Accra, Ghana
Mobile: +233 1234 567 890 Home: +233 000123456
Email: jgraham@abcd.com

PROFILE

An enthusiastic, dedicated and adaptable individual, **CIM qualified** with an HND in Marketing and valuable work experience within a variety of commercial environments. Self-motivated, hardworking and innovative; highly driven by the desire to achieve significant results, displaying a positive attitude, energy and good humour at all times. Performs well under pressure, with the ability to meet deadlines. A responsible and committed solutions provider, motivated by a challenge while working accurately and methodically.

CAREER OBJECTIVE

Looking to secure a challenging entry-level marketing role within a progressive environment with the opportunity for further self-development. Very keen to learn new skills and undertake further training.

KEY SKILLS

- **Communication & Interpersonal** – Strong interpersonal skills, effectively communicates across social and professional levels. Highly professional, with strong oral and written skills and an excellent telephone manner.
- **Problem Solving** – Analytical, applying initiative and creativity to complex issues. Able to act quickly and efficiently to resolve unexpected difficulties.
- **Critical Thinker** – Appreciates many perspectives, making sound decisions.
- **Customer Focus** – Able to engender trust, displaying absolute integrity in all transactions and relationships. Maintains a high quality of customer service and satisfaction, enhancing repeat and referral business.
- **Organisation & Prioritisation** – Plans, schedules and coordinates workload, able to multi-task and manage time effectively.
- **Administrative Management** – Prepares and maintains accurate documents and records.

CAREER HISTORY

Oct'05–Present   **ABC Retail Store, London**
                                  Part-time Cash Office Administrator

- Issue till floats and additional monies to sales staff to ensure smooth running of the business during busy trading periods
- Cash up and finalise tills at the end of the day
- Print off morning reports and complete banking procedures and financial reporting processes
- Report any losses to head office, successfully detecting a number of fraudulent cheques and avoiding significant losses to the company
- Record income and expenses, working meticulously and methodically, paying close attention to detail and investigating any discrepancies
- Reconcile extra floats and process vouchers via head office
- Improved audit procedures by running reports more regularly
- Separated the team into sub groups, each responsible for specific tasks in order to ensure realistic targets could be achieved

Jan'00–Mar'03   **BSA Bank, Accra, Ghana**
&Jan'04–May'04   **Assistant Customer Care Officer**

- Part-time role, providing general information on products to potential new customers
- Responded to general queries and complaints relating to accounts, interacting on a daily basis with customers face-to-face and by telephone and email, maximising any opportunities to improve service
- Introduced a system of recording and categorising customer complaints on the computor intranet system to ensure resolution within 24 hours, thus gaining a competitive edge within the local market
- Assisted Service and Recognition Manager with administrative tasks

- Assessed staff sales targets against objectives, teamwork, and customer care levels, making recommendations for internal achievement awards. Significantly decreased staff turnover and established an atmosphere of trust based upon mutual respect and shared objectives
- Issued bankers drafts, pension and sundry payments
- Organised overseas money transfers and dealt with returned cheques

2001   **JWS Commercial Bank – National Service**

- Provided petty banking, saving schemes to traders in designated market places
- Prospected for new clients for the bank, providing information about its products
- Assisted customers in opening and closing accounts

Sept'99–Jan'00   **ABD Union Assurance**
                           Assistant to Marketing Officer

- A part-time position, dealing with face-to-face and telephone customer enquiries
- Produced and presented reports on new customers, providing high quality after-sales care and completing administrative duties
- Visited private and commercial potential new customers and existing accounts to maintain strong business relations
- Commended for efforts in improving the quality of customer service contributing to a 3% increase in customer retention
- Conducted market research campaigns using questionnaires, telephone and the extranet to communicate with customers and staff

Jul'99–Oct'99   **CDA Broadcasting Corporation**

- A part-time position, responsible for prospecting new customers to buy air time for the radio station
- Assisted the marketing manager in identifying, developing and maintaining innovative programs for the radio station
- Wrote regular weekly reports

EDUCATION & TRAINING

Certificate in Corporate Banking & Financial Investment, 2006
Hackney Community College, London

CIM Post Graduate Certificate, 2006
London Bridge Business School, UK

CIM – Advanced and Certificate Level in Marketing, 2004
Institute of Professional Studies, Ghana

HND in Marketing, 2nd Class Upper, 2000
Kumasi Polytechnic, Ghana
Dissertation: Achieving Quality Customer Care Through Staff
(A case study of BCA Bank, Ghana)

Modules included: Customer Interface, Principles and practice of Selling, Marketing Management, Accounting Management for Marketers and International Marketing

8 SSCE (GCSE equivalent) including Mathematics and English

EXTRA CURRICULAR ACTIVITIES

1998–2001 Secretary of course association
Newsreader, campus radio station
1995–1997 Secretary of school drama group
Editorial Board Assistant of school magazine

IT SKILLS

Proficient user of MS Office 2000, Retail Java
Experienced in the use of email and the internet for research

INTERESTS

Enjoy sports, swimming, reading and taking part in any kind of personal development activities. Actively participated in raising funds and collecting goods for an orphanage in Ghana

CHAPTER 22

TOP CV TIPS

The following CV tips were devised by myself and are the advice and opinions of the 12 industry experts I interviewed:

1. Be truthful.
2. Let people get a feel for who you are.
3. Differentiate yourself from other candidates.
4. Invest a lot of time and energy into writing your CV.
5. Pay attention to layout and keep it simple.
6. Use bullet points as it makes your CV easy to read.
7. Be bold, be clear and show focus.
8. Each point must sell you in some way. If after reading a point you are left with the impression 'so what', remove it or improve it.
9. Avoid producing a job description; focus on your achievements.
10. Make positive statements and incorporate power words to strengthen them.
11. Use active words to enliven each point.
12. Make it very clear on the first page of your CV what your skills are and what you are offering.
13. Share your CV with professional advisors, family and friends.
14. Keep it concise and to no more than two/three pages.
15. Tailor your CV to the job being applied for or have multiple CVs.
16. Avoid using complicated words, acronyms and company jargon.
17. Provide a brief description of the companies you have worked for.
18. Ensure you provide all your contact information so that you can be contactcd easily.
19. Avoid being vague.

Part Three

Cover Letter Writing

INTRODUCTION: DON'T NEGLECT HOW IMPORTANT IT IS!

The importance of an accompanying cover letter is often overlooked. It is all very well to have a brilliant CV but if it not complemented by a cover letter, which adds a personal touch to a very factual document, you will be letting both yourself and your application down. Your cover letter should be an extension of your CV.

It is like going swimming but forgetting to take your trunks, or travelling abroad and forgetting to pack your passport.

If done correctly, a cover letter will most certainly set you apart from the competition. As with a CV, it must not be rushed and time must be allocated to producing a tailor-made letter for each application you make.

Two industry experts had the following comments to make:

> *People tend to make most of their mistakes on a cover letter.*
> *Sean Jowell at KPMG*

> *What you write in your cover letter can make or break your application.*
> *Anna Tomkins at Vodafone*

All the more reason to make sure you get it right!

The next four chapters stress the value of a cover letter and provide you with the tools you need to write a truly great one. Importantly they also include: mistakes that should be avoided and how to construct both speculative and tailor-made cover letters that will 'turn on' your specific audience. The final chapter comprises real life cover letters that have worked and is complemented by numerous cover letter examples provided on the appended CD.

CHAPTER 23

THE IMPORTANCE OF A COVER LETTER

Before we begin, it is important to define exactly what a cover letter is. A cover letter is an introductory letter that accompanies another document, in this instance your CV, and it provides additional information.

Essentially, a cover letter has two purposes: one, to ensure your CV is read and two, to ask for an interview. You thus need to ensure that you give your cover letter the time and attention it deserves as it can be the making or breaking of whether or not you are invited to interview.

More reasons to use a cover letter:
- A cover letter introduces you as an individual and provides you with an opportunity to present your character and personality to a prospective employer before speaking with them.
- It provides you with an opportunity to expand on the information provided in your CV.
- It shows that you are serious about the opportunity.
- It demonstrates good communication and organisational skills.
- If done properly, it can set you apart from other applicants and dramatically improve your chances of being invited to interview.
- It provides you with a further chance to sell yourself.

A cover letter is also a useful tool as it can be used to:
- Instil your passion for the role and the company.
- Elaborate on your current and future goals.
- Explain specific circumstances that may have affected past or future performance.
- Add additional information that is relevant to the position being applied for but is not included on your CV.

198

THE VALUE OF A COVER LETTER

Most people will spend many, many hours constructing their CV. It is surprising though how many of these people overlook the importance of the document that should accompany and introduce their CV, i.e. the cover letter.

In a market that is becoming more and more competitive, neglecting to include a cover letter is a big mistake. Industry experts who shared my views had this to say:

> *I think cover letters are essential. A cover letter is your opportunity to show that you have done some research, that you have understood what the company is about, what its products/services are, demonstrated interest in that company, an opportunity to tell that company what you can bring to them.*
>
> *Daniell Morrisey at the BBC*

> *I think a cover letter is important because I think it can give the recruiter a much clearer idea on specifically your interests and why you think you're appropriate for the job. So, I think a skilfully crafted cover letter would say, 'this is clearly the job that I'm applying for or the entry point in your organisation I am interested in, and this is why I think you should consider me'.*
>
> *Mark Thomas at Tesco*

Two industry experts interviewed felt a cover letter adds little or no value. This is what they had to say on the subject:

> *I don't see what value a cover letter brings. [A CV should be concise and contain all the relevant information]. I normally scan through cover letters and I'm seldom surprised by them; they normally say the same thing, 'Oh, I'm so interested, I'm such a great person to work with, and you're such a great company'.*
>
> *Adrian Cojocaru at Mars Drinks*

> *Generally not all that important in my opinion. If the CV has the right ingredients then that on its own will generally do the job. It's very seldom in my experience that a cover letter has somehow trumped a CV in terms of really materially influencing a decision on whether to hire or interview a candidate.*
>
> Jonathan Jones at Goldman Sachs

Personally, I think Jonathan and Adrian are expressing views on cover letters they have seen that have not had that 'wow' factor. I agree that if you cannot wow your audience, then you are doing yourself an injustice by including a cover letter and it could be the breaking of your application. You may be now feeling concerned and wondering, 'well, what if I get it wrong and blow all the hard work I have done on my CV', fear not! Art can be copied and there are many, many examples of real-life letters that have worked.

I stress again that a CV is a factual document. A cover letter provides you with an opportunity to add a personal touch and to sell yourself further. Furthermore, should you be responding to a specific role, a cover letter allows you to express your interest in the company and the role, and summarise why you would be a good fit. In the case of a speculative approach, you can express what type of role you are looking for, what you can bring to their organisation and what appeals to you about working for them as an organisation. This is not something that can be included on your CV.

Most experts agreed that when applying speculatively, a cover letter is imperative as recruiters want to know what role you are interested in, why their company appeals to you and how you have come to them. Anna Tomkins at Vodafone adds:

> *It's important to work out who to target in that company. For large organisations such as Vodafone, there's no point in writing to the Chief Executive or the HR Director. Work out how to apply.*
>
> Anna Tomkins at Vodafone

Another important point: research the organisations that you are applying to and adapt how you apply. If you are applying for a specific role, always follow the process they have asked you to follow. If you are given the option on whether or not to include a cover letter, which you often are with online applications, it is a judgement call as to whether to include one or not.

> *If you are trying to move into a different type of role with transferable skills, it would be a really good opportunity to include a cover letter if it's optional because there's a way of explaining something that might not necessarily be obvious on your CV. Whereas, if you're in that role already and actually just looking for your next step up, if a cover letter is optional, then I think you don't necessarily need one because your CV is going to speak for itself; it's a judgement call.*
>
> *Anna Tomkins at Vodafone*

If you are given the option to include one, I recommend that you do, and ensure it is bespoke. Each cover letter you write needs to be tailored to the role and the company. What irks HR professionals more than anything is when they receive a generic cover letter, i.e. a letter where it would be very easy to replace their company name with another company's name.

> *Some candidates use very standard letters that look almost like a script – they are not very personalised and they do not relate to the actual job that has been advertised. That is fine because they are probably using this letter to apply for 50 jobs and they may not have the time to write a separate cover letter for each job. Rather than apply for 50 jobs and only give it 40 or 50% of your effort, it is better to use 100% effort and apply to 10 jobs and make sure you get it right each time. This way candidates will have a much higher chance of getting called up for interview.*
>
> *Sean O'Donoghue at Jonathan Wren*

The next chapter covers top tips for writing a good cover letter.

CHAPTER 24

THE MARKS OF A GOOD COVER LETTER

Having read Chapter 23, I trust that you now agree that a cover letter is a necessary evil. I refer to them in this light as they are time consuming; they must be tailored for each role. Just as every job or company has a different set of criteria, your cover letter also needs to detail a different set of criteria. If you do not get it right, all the hard work you have put into your CV will be for nothing. A poorly constructed or non-existent cover letter may result in your CV be binned before it has even been read.

This chapter comprises six top tips of what to do and three tips of what not to do to make sure you do get it right.

THE MARKS OF A GOOD COVER LETTER

1. Personalise your letter

Your letter MUST be personally addressed to someone by name. If you want someone to spend time reading your letter, afford them the same courtesy by showing you have taken the time to research the correct addressee. More often than not, all it takes is one simple phone call to find out the correct contact. This shows that you have taken time to research the role, it displays interest and it also allows you to then follow up your application.

> *Make sure you have contacted the company and researched who the correct person is; double check you have the spelling correct, get the address correct and address it to the right sex.*
>
> Daniell Morrisey at the BBC

So, if someone has a unisex name like Pat or Jamie, make sure you get their sex right. Also ensure that you spell both their first name and surname correctly. There is nothing more disgruntling for some people if you get either of these wrong.

> *"To whom it might concern" might appear a little bit lazy.*
>
> Jonathan Jones at Goldman Sachs

> *If you end up going the 'Dear Sir' or 'Dear Madam' route, you never know where you're going to end up; in a large organisation that can be a problem.*
>
> Mark Thomas at Tesco

2. Well laid out and constructed

- Make reference to the vacancy that you are applying for.
- Your letter must be laid out as a standard business letter with your name, address and contact number.
- Do not be tempted to use headers or personal logos.
- Keep the tone professional.
- Your letter should not be more than one page long. Keep words, sentences and paragraphs short. It is recommended that there should be no more than four or five paragraphs, or 200 words.

3. Address the criteria that the position advertises

If you are responding to a specific role:

- keep the content relevant and as targeted as possible;
- quickly explain what you have to offer;
- summarise your experience and achievements relevant to the job being applied for;
- highlight the most important points from your CV. Be careful not to copy sentences direct from your CV as repetition reduces the impact of your letter;
- identify what skills they require and provide demonstrable examples for each of these.

> *' The covering letter should describe who you are, where you've come from and to whom you might be useful. '*
>
> Will Dawkins at Odgers, Ray and Berndtson

If you are applying speculatively:

- express what role you are looking for or the entry point in the company;
- quickly explain what you have to offer;
- summarise your experience and achievements relevant to your target position;
- highlight the most important points from your CV. Be careful not to copy sentences direct from your CV as repetition reduces the impact of your letter;
- research the company to identify what skills they look for in a typical employee and provide demonstrable examples of each skill.

4. Show enthusiasm for the company and the role

- Demonstrate an understanding of the company by showing that you have spent time researching the company, its products, services and markets. Explain what you know and like about them as this helps to build rapport with the reader and displays enthusiasm for the company and the role.
- If you know anything about the reader's background or achievements, express that here.
- Persuade the employer that you are confident that you can do the job, and convey enthusiasm.
- Leave the employer wanting more.

> *' A cover letter should say 'this is me, this is who I am, this is what I can add to your company and this is why you should employ me'. It has to move naturally into the CV to give the employer the interest to want to read it. '*
>
> Sean O'Donoghue at Jonathan Wren

5. Reason for writing

It is imperative, particularly when approaching large, multi-faceted organisations, to specify what kind of role you are looking to be considered for and in what area. Too often, the onus is on HR to work it out. In summary, it needs to be clear in terms of its purpose.

6. Let your cover letter help you stand out

Wow your audience using unique selling points and/or impressive achievements. Express how you could solve a potential problem they may be having and/or what the impact of hiring you would be. Leave the reader wanting more and eager to invite you to interview.

Daniell Morrisey at the BBC provides an example of how this can be achieved:

> *In the creative industries, our currency is ideas, so for example, if you were applying for a job on a magazine, why not suggest a feature idea?*
> *Daniell Morrisey at the BBC*

MISTAKES THAT SHOULD BE AVOIDED

- As with a CV, your cover letter must be double and triple checked to ensure there are no spelling mistakes or grammatical errors. Spelling and grammatical errors are not tolerated as they say one of three things – no attention-to-detail, poor command of the English Language, or no professionalism.
- Avoid sending a letter that looks like it has been mass mailed. This will irk a prospective employer rather than achieving what a cover letter should do – make you stand out!
- Do not apply for a role that you are clearly unqualified for or have little or none of the competencies they require. You will be wasting both your time and that of the prospective employer.

FOLLOWING UP YOUR APPLICATION

Should you convey that you will follow up your application with a phone call?

This is an area where you need to make a judgement call. It is very much down to the preference of the individual handling the recruitment campaign. Some of those interviewed viewed it as being proactive and showing initiative whilst others perceived it as being 'too forward'.

In larger organisations where HR departments receive several thousand applications each year, they would probably be less responsive to this approach. More often than not they have certain protocols they have to follow, and consequently, they will get back to you either way.

> ❛ If you've got a good CV and you're interested in the organisation, an organisation will contact you if they are interested in you. ❜
>
> *Mark Thomas at Tesco*

My opinion would be to follow up your application if it is a role you are deeply passionate about or if you are confident that there is likely to be a small response. If you do choose to include a follow-up date in your letter, make sure that the date is one week to 10 days after the closing date of the application. If you are applying speculatively then make your follow-up date one week to 10 days after sending your application. If you do state that you will follow up your application, then it is imperative that you do so.

CHAPTER 25

SPECULATIVE VERSUS SPECIFIC COVER LETTERS

Having read the previous two chapters, you should appreciate the importance of a cover letter, what should be included in a cover letter and what mistakes should be avoided. Before we begin discussing how to construct a cover letter, it is important to differentiate between the two types:

Speculative letter: A letter used when you are writing to a company to establish what opportunities may exist for someone with your skills and experience.

Specific letter: A letter in response to a specific vacancy that has been advertised or is on offer.

Each letter will now be discussed in detail and examples will be used at each stage in the process.

SPECULATIVE COVER LETTERS

We all admire or respect a wide array of companies and sometimes reflect on how great it would be to work for a company like them! There is nothing to stop you writing to them to establish what opportunities they may have for someone with your skills and experience. It is a good way of opening lines of communication and actually, most companies are very open to receiving applications on spec as it not only gives them a good source of candidates to fill roles that they are recruiting for now or in the future, but it may also save them expensive agency or headhunting fees.

When writing to a company, be very specific about the type of role or roles you are interested in and in which area(s) you are looking to work. To send your application to a busy HR department and specify that you are looking to be considered for any roles they are presently recruiting for is not very helpful. Make their lives as easy as possible and you are more likely to be rewarded for your efforts.

Articulate why the company appeals to you. Rather than saying that you are interested in them because they are compelling and dynamic, try to demonstrate that you have done your homework by mentioning what it is exactly about that company that appeals to you and if you can find any information on the reader themselves, even better. It builds rapport and shows enthusiasm. Companies have been known to create positions for the right applicant.

As mentioned in the previous chapter, do not produce a generic letter that clearly shows that you have not taken the time to do any research about the company. It is fine to have a generic letter but it is necessary to tweak it each time it is sent out to ensure it is as targeted as possible.

Constructing a speculative cover letter

1. Opening paragraph

- In the first sentence of the opening paragraph, express your reason for writing and if appropriate, detail what area or industry you are interested in.
- The next sentence should explain why the company appeals to you. This is your opportunity to show that you have done your research.
- The last sentence of the first paragraph should outline what position or positions you are interested in.

Example 1:

I have been researching the market for dynamic, forward thinking companies specialising in <area of interest>. <Company name> has an impressive track record for <provide details> and I am writing to establish whether you have any opportunities for a <job title>.

Example 2:

<Company name> is a company that I have followed closely over the years for <reason>. Having successfully <provide a recent achievement>, I am now seeking to secure a new and challenging <job title> role. Consequently, I am writing to establish whether you currently have any suitable opportunities.

Example 3: As a result of a relocation

I will be immigrating to <country name> in <Month>, and as such, I have been researching the <country name> market for <company description>. <Company name> has a reputation for <details> and I would value the opportunity to work for an esteemed organisation such as yours. Consequently, I am writing to establish whether you require the services of a <job title>.

Example 4:

I am currently studying at the University of XYZ and will be graduating with a <provide name of degree> in <month>. My particular interests lie within <list interests> and I am presently seeking a position where I would have the opportunity to work within this exciting field. Please find attached my Curriculum Vitae for any roles you are presently resourcing in <list department or area>.

Example 5: Application to an agency or executive search firm

<Company name> has a superb reputation for working with and placing <job titles>. I am now eager to embark on a new challenge and I am writing to establish whether your clients may have a need for a <provide summary of experience>.

2. Body
- In the next paragraph, summarise your experience and articulate your most relevant experience in relation to the role(s) you are interested in.
- Next, list two or three achievements that would provide the reader with an insight into what the business benefit of hiring you would be. Provide them with a reason to contact you or worst case scenario, keep your CV on file. Paraphrase your achievements; ensure you do not copy them directly from your CV.

- Review the company's website in order to ascertain what they look for in a potential employee. Then, convey those skills that will be of particular interest to the company and where appropriate, provide examples of where these skills have been demonstrated.
- Explain your interest in them as a company and what you feel you could bring to the organisation/department.
- Finally, what can you offer that is special or unique?

Example 1:

With over <xx> years' experience as a <job title>, I have a wealth of experience of <list core experience> in a highly demanding environment, coupled with <provide details of other areas of strength>.

My career highlights include <list two/three achievements> . . .

I possess strong <list one/two core skills> with a proven ability to <provide examples of how/where you have demonstrated these skills>.

I am recognised for <unique selling point>.

Example 2:

You will see from my enclosed CV that I am an experienced <job title> with <summarise experience>.

In my most recent roles, I have utilised my skills and experience to <list specific examples of where you have demonstrated your skills>.

I am a performance driven individual with a proven record of achievement of <provide details of two or three achievements>.

Example 3:

I am a career driven, enthusiastic individual/graduate with a <list education details> from <name of university/college/school>. During my studies, I have found <name subjects> to be the most rewarding, and would be very eager to begin my training in one of these disciplines.

Having worked as a <job title> during the summer, I gained valuable commercial experience which has provided me with an invaluable insight into <elaborate on experience gained>. Additionally, I honed <list skills that they are likely to be looking for in a graduate>.

Whilst at school/college/university <list details of some of your responsibilities or achievements, anything that will provide a prospective employer with an insight into what your capabilities are>.

3. Concluding your letter
- In one/two sentences summarise what you feel you can bring to the company or department.
- State when follow up will be, if appropriate.
- Convey your interest in hearing from them and thank them for their time.

Example 1:

As someone who is <summarise core strengths>, I am confident that I would make a valuable contribution to <company name or department/ team name>. I would welcome the opportunity to discuss my application further and will call you on <date> to establish how best to progress my application.

Example 2:

I am particularly interested in a <job title> position as I believe that the combination of <list your strengths, main skills and experience>, will make a positive contribution to the success and profitability of <company name>. I would be delighted to discuss my application in more detail and I will contact you on <date> to establish a suitable time for a meeting.

Example 3:

As an enthusiastic, goal-driven individual, I believe that I can bring a fresh, innovative approach to <company name/department>. I would welcome the opportunity to discuss my application further and I look forward to hearing from you soon.

SPECIFIC COVER LETTERS

Specific letters should be used to respond to an advertisement or in response to an approach by a company, agency or head-hunter. Perhaps you have been made aware of an opportunity through a friend or colleague or maybe it is an internal vacancy.

Constructing a specific cover letter

1. Reference

Where appropriate, make reference to the role you are applying for. When responding to an advertisement, there is often a job reference number. If no reference number has been supplied, make reference to the role they are seeking to fill.

A reference should appear directly after 'Dear Name'.

Example 1:

Dear Mrs Allan

REF: Job reference 34215

Example 2:

Dear Mrs Allan

RE: Vacancy for a Marketing Director

2. Opening paragraph

- Express your reason for writing; include the title of the job and how you became aware of the vacancy.
- Next, express your interest in the company and the opportunity, and convey your knowledge about the company or reader.

The scenario will determine how you start your letter.

Example 1: In response to an advertisement

<Company name> is a consultancy that I highly respect and admire as you have a reputation for <provide details>. I am also attracted to your organisation as you are known for rewarding hard work and nurturing talent. Following your advertisement in the <name of publication> on <date>, I am writing to apply for the position of <job title>.

Example 2: In response to an advertisement

In response to your advertisement for a <job title> placed in the <name of publication> on <date>, I am writing to apply for the position. <Company name> is a company <elaborate on why you admire or respect them> and I would relish the opportunity to work for your organisation. I have attached my CV for your consideration.

Example 3: In response to an advertisement

Being a dedicated and highly diligent student, I am incredibly keen to develop my education by means of a summer internship with a prominent <industry> organisation such as yours. I consider myself to have all the experience and attributes that you are looking for, for the position of <job title>, which my enclosed CV will attest.

Example 4: In response to a contact

<Company name> is an organisation that I hold in high regard and hence my elation to be contacted by <contact name>, who advised me that you presently have an opening for a <job title>. I am confident that I have all the skills and experience you are looking for and I am pleased to attach my CV for your perusal.

Example 4: In response to an internal vacancy

Following the recent retirement of <person's name>, <person's name, job title> recommended that I apply for the position as <job title>. Having worked for <company name> since <year>, I have <expand on your understanding of the company and the role>. As my enclosed CV will attest, I have all the skills and experience that you are looking for and this would be a natural step up for me.

2. Body

- In the first paragraph, summarise your experience and skills most relevant to the role you are applying for.
- The advertisement will list certain criteria and job requirements; the proceeding paragraphs should detail how you satisfy or exceed those requirements.
- Paraphrase two or thee of your achievements that will provide a prospective employer with assurance of your ability to do this job.

- Clarify you interest in their company and what you feel you could bring to the organisation/department.
- Finally, what can you offer that is special or unique?

Example 1:

As you will see from my enclosed CV, I was <job title> at <company name> where I was responsible for the <list main duties and responsibilities>. I have many years experience in <elaborate on your areas of expertise>, which I feel uniquely qualify me for this job opportunity.

Besides undertaking <demonstrate your experience and qualifications in relation to the role>, I have recently qualified as <qualification> and am educated to degree level.

I enjoy working in the <name of industry> industry and feel I am capable of developing excellent rapport with the people I work with. <Provide details of what skills and strengths you have in relation to the job being applied for and provide examples of where you have demonstrated these skills>.

In addition to my knowledge of <areas of expertise>, I have other qualities that will help me succeed in your organisation. I have developed the ability to <provide details of other areas of strength>.

Example 2: In response to an agency/head-hunting firm

I note the requirements of the role and am confident that my experience and abilities would enable me to make a valuable contribution to your client.

Currently employed by <company name> as a <job title>, I have <xx> years' progressive experience of <state your core competencies and strengths in relation to the role>. Additionally, I am recognised as <provide further abilities in relation to target position>.

My most recent achievements have included <provide two/three achievements that demonstrate your abilities to perform this kind of role for a similar organisation>.

I am <expand on further skills and experience that have been requested in the job specification and provide examples of where these skills have been displayed>.

Example 3:

I am an enthusiastic, committed graduate who has recently completed a <details of degree>. Having successfully completed internships last year and studied intensively this year, I have developed a sound understanding of <elaborate on experience and knowledge gained that is relevant to the role being applied for>. This has been reinforced by my participation in extra curricular activities and my consequent flourishing achievements.

Being a <list some of your key attributes relevant to the role> individual with exceptional <list two/three skills necessary for the job in question (e.g. communication and financial skills)>, I would benefit from fresh challenges and be able to integrate well within your organisation, interacting with clients and personnel at all levels.

Furthermore, <list any achievements whilst at school, university or college that demonstrate skills that they are requesting>.

3. Concluding your letter

- End the letter by reiterating your desire for the role and the company, and your confidence in your suitability for it.
- Express when follow up will be, if applicable.
- Convey your interest in hearing from and working with them.

Example 1:

I am confident that my skills and vast experience of <summarise your experience> will provide a pivotal platform for undertaking this interesting and demanding role. I would welcome the opportunity to discuss my application further and will call you on <date> to establish when our schedules will permit a face-to-face meeting.

Example 2:

In summary, I am attracted to the variety that this role will afford me and I would relish the challenge. As a result of my <elaborate on experience>, I firmly believe that I would make a valuable long-term contribution to <company name>. I would welcome the opportunity to meet with you and will call you on <date> to arrange a suitable time.

Example 3:

The honour of an internship with <company name> would hone my existing knowledge and experience whilst providing a more detailed insight into the world of <industry>. I am confident that I would offer a valuable contribution to <company name> and would welcome the opportunity to attend an interview.

Example 4:

With a studious disposition, entrepreneurial flair and with the capacity to easily absorb knowledge, I am confident that I am equipped to undertake any task presented in a professional and efficient manner. I would value the opportunity to discuss my application in more detail and I look forward to hearing from you.

Example 5: Internal opportunity

Having worked for <company name> for several years and closely with <person's name>, I have carried out many functions of the role in question and I feel that this would be a natural next step for me. I am highly passionate about <company name> <expand on why>, and I am confident that I would excel as the new <job title> due to my ability <list one/two reasons>. I would welcome the opportunity to discuss my application further and I will call you on <date> to discuss.

SUMMARY

- Personalise your letter.
- Keep it professional and concise.
- Express your reason for writing.
- Demonstrate a knowledge of the company as this helps to build rapport with your reader and displays enthusiasm.
- Explain your background, experience and how you can contribute to the company at this particular time.
- Summarise your experience. Include your most relevant skills and emphasise your most significant achievements i.e., those most appropriate to the job being applied for.
- Highlight the most important points from your CV. A cover letter needs to complement your CV and should never duplicate information from your CV, so reword sentences – do not copy sentences verbatim from your CV.
- Persuade the employer that you are confident you can do the job.
- Convey enthusiasm as enthusiasm sells.
- Keep the content relevant to your target position.
- Explain what appeals to you about both the role and the company.
- Provide demonstrable examples of what you can bring to the company and what the benefit in hiring someone like you would be.
- State when follow up will be. This will help set you apart from other applicants and will show your enthusiasm for the role. But, you MUST then follow up.

For full examples of both speculative and specific cover letters, please refer to the next chapter and to the attached CD.

CHAPTER 26

SPECIFIC COVER LETTERS THAT HAVE WORKED

If you get your cover letter right, you will dramatically increase your chances of being invited to interview. The purpose of this chapter is to provide you with an appreciation of how to analyse a job specification, advertisement or similar; the art of mirroring; and how to go about constructing an interview-winning cover letter based on what is required. Four real-life examples of specific cover letters that have been successful are explored and analysed.

Recruiters screening CVs do not always fully understand the role they are trying to fill. They are working from a hiring authority's wish list of what their ideal candidate is and this is what the recruiter has to work with. Your job is to make their job as simple as possible; this means ensuring that your relevant skills and experience stand out on your cover letter. This way, you significantly increase your chances of being short-listed.

Each of the four examples will now be discussed in detail. In each scenario, you are provided with the original job specification (which has been changed slightly to protect the identity of the company), the cover letter that was prepared, and finally a commentary of why the letter worked. In each example you will note that the focus is on emphasising skills and experience in relation to the person specification.

The first two examples are in response to an advertisement; the third is in response to an internal vacancy; the fourth and final example is a letter written by a candidate looking to be accepted onto a course.

EXAMPLE 1: ANDREA SMITH

Andrea is seeking to secure a graduate trainee position with a major investment bank or hedge fund. An executive search firm has been retained to identify potential candidates on behalf of their client and Andrea needs to convince the search firm that she is the right candidate for the programme.

Job title: Graduate Programme

Company: Alexander Executive Search Ltd

Job description: The individual will create and compile presentations for clients; examine data and trends within the emerging market space specifically investment banking activity. A substantial portion of our transactions are cross border and the role will include travel to our key markets including Moscow, Istanbul, Dubai, Warsaw and Athens.

Person requirements: To be considered the candidate must have an exceptional academic background, strong communication and presentation skills, be charismatic, entrepreneurial and a team player. Proficiency in relevant languages is required, as this individual will be expected to help service Emerging markets based clients. Should have strong knowledge of Microsoft Office; in particular Excel, Word and Visio.

Vacancy type: Permanent

Job status: Full-time

Closing date: 20/05/200X

How to apply: Leading City-Based Boutique Financial Services Emerging Markets specialist Executive Search firm is looking for strong individuals to join the graduate training programme.

The firm works on a retainer basis for top tier Investment Banks & Hedge Funds within Emerging markets.

With offices based in London, Moscow and Dubai key areas of regional coverage are:

* Russia/CIS
* MENA/GCC
* Central & Eastern Europe
* Turkey, Greece & Southern Europe
* Sub-Saharan Africa

Assistance in obtaining a UK work permit will be offered to successful candidates if necessary.

This firm has one of the most competitive remuneration structures in the City whereby commission is based on individual and team based performance.

Alexander Executive Search Ltd

Tel: 0123 456 789

Email: gp@abcd.com

Breaking down what is required as per the job specification

The candidate **must have**:

- ■ an exceptional academic background;
- ■ strong communication and presentation skills.

The candidate **must be**:

- ■ charismatic, entrepreneurial and a team player;
- ■ proficient in relevant languages.

The candidate **should have**:

- ■ strong knowledge of Microsoft Office; in particular Excel, Word and Visio.

It is essential that all the 'must haves' be covered, followed by the 'nice to haves'. As mentioned in previous chapters, if there is something you do not have, do not draw attention to it. Remember, this is the specification for the company's IDEAL candidate.

The next page provides the actual copy of the letter that Andrea sent as an accompaniment to her CV.

Ms Andrea Smith
3 No Name Street
Oxford
OX2

1 May 200X

Mr John Greene
Consultant
Alexander Executive Search Ltd
25 Fleet Street
London
EC4 1AB

Ref: **Graduate Programme**

Dear Mr Greene,

I am very interested in joining your client's Graduate Programme. I have been looking to secure a challenging and exciting trainee position within an internationally focused and dynamic organisation, where I might have the opportunity to progress and develop my skills. I enclose my Curriculum Vitae for your consideration.

I possess excellent academic credentials, as a graduate in Law and Business Management with an MBA in International Business and Finance. Currently I am studying towards a Master's Degree in European Studies at a leading business school, which I will complete later this year.

During my studies, I have had the opportunity to work with several Romanian organisations and successfully developed financial and x-efficiency programmes with them. I possess local connections within Eastern Europe (specifically the Russian and Romanian markets). I aspire to become a leader within an international business environment and feel that my language skills and understanding of other business cultures will be a great advantage as I enter the marketplace.

I am determined, confident and ambitious, with high levels of both academic and non-academic achievements. My communication and interpersonal skills are of a very high quality; I am diplomatic and good-humoured, maintaining a positive and supportive attitude with the ability to achieve desired results. I work well under pressure and excel in planning and organisation. A critical thinker, I am a highly capable decision-maker with excellent analytical and problem solving skills. My IT skills are strong, as well as my ability to confidently present information clearly and concisely to an audience.

I possess a genuine passion for business and some knowledge of the investment markets. I place a high value upon teamwork and the development of good working relationships with colleagues and clients. I enjoy travel and would embrace the opportunity to work internationally and work with global business leaders.

I feel that my experience and abilities would provide a positive influence within a forward thinking organisation and I would welcome the opportunity to discuss my interest further. Should you require any further information please do not hesitate to contact me.

Yours sincerely

Andrea Smith
Enc CV

Analysing the letter

Andrea begins her letter by expressing her interest in the organisation; even though she does not know who the client is, she draws upon some small details provided in the job specification.

In the second paragraph of her letter, Andrea quickly matches one of the core credentials – academic achievement and provides detail of her qualifications.

As the company has global operations, she then goes on to highlight her international experience with emerging markets and her international connections. She continues in the same vein by drawing attention to the fact that she is multilingual and has had exposure to multi-cultural environments.

In the fourth and fifth paragraphs, she covers the two final requirements being computer literacy and her ability to work as part of a team.

She concludes the letter by expressing what she feels she can bring to the client and ultimately what the benefit to hiring her would be.

Conclusion

All in all, Andrea expressed why she was a strong contender for this position and matched her skills and experience closely to the job specification, being sure to cover off each point. It is not surprising to hear that she was invited for interview.

EXAMPLE 2: SHIRLEY SIMONS

Shirley was applying for a role as a Guidelines Commissioning Manager in the public sector.

ABC NATIONAL INSTITUTE

Person Specification

Job Title	Guidelines Commissioning Manager
Team/Area of Work	Centre for Clinical Practice
Centre/Directorate	Centre for Clinical Practice

Knowledge, training and qualifications	
1. Requires highly developed specialist knowledge across the range of work procedures and practices underpinned by theoretical knowledge and relevant practical experience. • Masters degree or Doctorate, or • Equivalent level of knowledge acquired through experience and further training/development.	Essential
2. Familiarity with methodological approaches used to develop clinical guidelines or services.	Desirable
3. High level of interpersonal skills.	Essential
4. Ability to demonstrate the skills necessary to establish effective working relationships with a range of external organisations.	Essential
5. Ability to analyse complex issues, to think and plan strategically and to exercise sound judgement in the face of conflicting pressures.	Essential
6. Ability to deploy resources effectively.	Essential
7. Understanding of the social, political, economic and technological context in which the NHS operates.	Essential
8. An understanding of equal opportunities and the meaning of valuing diversity.	Essential

Experience	
9. Experience of managing clinical services in an operational unit or commissioning in the NHS.	Desirable
10. Experience of designing and leading on the implementation of significant change in clinical practice or service organisation, ideally across NHS units, within a local health community.	Desirable
11. Experience of managing project budgets.	Desirable
12. Experience of methodologies used in guideline development, e.g. literature searching, systematic reviewing, consensus methods and group working.	Desirable
13. Experience in working with a range of stakeholders in a health care setting.	Desirable
14. Ability to use standard Microsoft packages (including Word, Excel, PowerPoint, Access, Outlook) and websites.	Essential
Other attributes	
15. Effective and persuasive communicator demonstrating oral, written and presentation skills, with a high degree of personal credibility.	Essential
16. Initiative and judgement to be able to advise the Guideline Review Panels and the Centre Director on matters relating to the development of clinical guidelines.	Essential
17. Ability to engage effectively with clinical, academic and managerial colleagues.	Essential

Breaking down what is required as per the job specification

In the job specification it clearly states what is 'essential' and what is 'desirable'. As such it is important that Shirley specifies her experience and skills in relation to what is required.

The next page provides the actual copy of the letter that Shirley sent as an accompaniment to her CV.

Ms Shirley Simons
No 3 Apple Tree Road
Winchester SO53
Tel: 07123456 789
2 May 200X

Mr Andrew Warton
Associate Director
ABC National Institute (ABCNI)
21 Short Road
London, WC1 5TA

Dear Mr Warton

Ref: Guidelines Commissioning Manager Vacancy

ABCNI is well known for providing independent, authoritative and reliable advice on healthcare issues. I have followed your organisation closely over the years and have been involved in the implementation of the ABCNI guideline for schizophrenia. As such, I have had first-hand experience of embedding ABCNI guidance into clinical practice.

In response to your advertisement for a Guidelines Commissioning Manager, I attach my CV for your consideration. I am a health professional with many years' experience working in the NHS. Additionally, I am from a nursing background and as such, I have the clinical experience, knowledge and maturity to understand the challenges that comes with a fluid organisation such as the NHS.

I possess self awareness, am politically aware and I have good analytical capabilities. I am an accomplished manager with a strong leadership ability and a demonstrable track record of managing the full lifecycle of several successful NHS projects.

My key skills and experience in relation to the role advertised are:
- currently studying towards a masters degree in Trans-cultural Mental Health;
- a skilled, persuasive communicator with well-developed interpersonal skills;
- effectively engaging with colleagues from various professional backgrounds;
- experience of working with a range of stakeholders in the healthcare arena;
- adept at presenting complex information to multidisciplinary teams;
- familiar with methodological approaches used to develop clinical guidance;
- a thorough understanding of the social, political, economic and technological context in which the NHS operates;
- designing and leading the implementation of significant change in the NHS.

My most recent achievement was leading the development of the physical healthcare policy for my Trust. I recruited and chaired the strategy group, balancing the needs of various professional groups whilst keeping the physical healthcare objectives at the forefront. Currently, I am managing the consultation process for the policy, and identifying and communicating with stakeholders through various means. The policy is due to be launched within budget and on time.

I am passionate about improving patient care and raising standards, and as ABCNI is a learning organisation, I believe you would benefit from the level of experience and knowledge that I can offer to enhance your commitment to high quality clinical care. ABCNI exemplifies quality and excellence, which mirrors my career aspirations and is what motivates me.

It would be an honour to work for ABCNI, a highly pre-eminent organisation in the world of healthcare, and I would welcome the opportunity to discuss my application in more detail. I will call you on 16 May 200X to have an informal discussion. In the meantime, please do not hesitate to contact me.

Yours sincerely

Shirley Simons BSc (Hons)

Analysing the letter

Importantly, the letter has been personalised and addressed to someone specific, i.e. Mr Andrew Warton. This not only shows that Shirley has taken time to research the company, it adds a personal touch and it also allows her to follow up her application.

Shirley begins her letter by demonstrating an understanding for and an interest in the company she is applying to. Skilfully, she also expresses previous exposure she has had with the company concerned.

She goes on to summarise her experience and background in relation to the role to which she is applying. In the third paragraph, she highlights some of her skills that are essential in order to perform the job and expands on her project management experience.

In paragraph four she expresses all of her skills and experience in relation to the job specification, making it very easy for a reader to see that she meets the criteria.

She subsequently highlights one of her most recent achievements, accentuating her ability to perform this role; it demonstrates the fact that she has achieved something similar for a previous employer.

Paragraphs five and six summarise what she can bring to the role and why the company and role appeal to her.

She concludes her letter by stating that she will follow up her application in two weeks' time. This shows she is proactive and again displays enthusiasm for the opportunity.

Conclusion

This letter was well laid out and it covered all the points raised in the specification, making it easy for the person screening applications to quickly see that Shirley met the minimum criteria as laid out by the job specification. It also demonstrates that even though she was missing one key element, i.e. research methodology (which note, she did not draw attention to), she was still invited to interview.

At interview, they were impressed with her wealth of experience in the NHS and felt that she was personable with good interpersonal skills. Generally the interview went well but unfortunately she did not get the job due to weakness in the area of research methodology; which was one of the essential criteria. They have invited Shirley to re-apply once she has completed her master's degree.

EXAMPLE 3 – AIDAN REDBOURN

Aidan currently works as a Production Manager at XYZ Dairy's Shipley site. He is now seeking to secure an internal position as Purchasing Planning Manager.

The specification appears on the next page.

XYZ DAIRY

PURCHASING PLANNING MANAGER

XYZ Dairy is a successful, expanding, independent cheese company, operating in the retail sector, dealing with leading UK and global companies.

We are looking to recruit a Purchasing Planning Manager, the role to include:

Purchasing – To ensure that the company obtains the most competitive purchase prices for raw materials, packaging and other items by means of contract negotiation for others to order against that are commensurate with quality, technical and company purchasing strategy.

To ensure that stocks, goods and services are properly controlled, managed and accounted for at all locations so that they are available for use when required.

Planning – Responsible for accurate planning and forecasting you will play a vital role within the business ensuring efficient production, product quality and the highest levels of customer service via efficient purchasing, just-in-time management, stock control and good general operational planning.

Candidate – The ideal candidate will have experience in a purchasing/planning role in the food manufacturing industry, with chilled food experience. You will have excellent communication and negotiation skills, together with a 'hands-on' approach, able to plan and organise your workload effectively and have good IT skills.

If you are interested in this role
please pass your expression of interest to:
Kathy Henderson, Operations Manager by Friday 16 May

Breaking down what is required as per the job specification

The candidate **must have**:

- experience in a purchasing/planning role in the food manufacturing industry, with chilled food experience;
- excellent communication and negotiation skills;
- a 'hands-on' approach;
- an ability to plan and organise workload effectively;
- good IT skills.

The next page provides the actual copy of the letter that Aidan sent as an accompaniment to his CV.

Aidan Redbourn
20 Apple Tree Lane
Liverpool
L8

Tel: 07123 456 789

2 May 200X

Kathy Henderson
Operations Manager
XYZ Dairy Limited
25 Baron Road
Liverpool
L7

Dear Mrs Henderson,

Ref: Purchasing Planning Manager

I am writing with reference to the vacancy for the position of **Purchasing Planning Manager**, and enclose my Curriculum Vitae for your consideration. I am a highly experienced manufacturing management professional, keen to further apply my skills and experience to the benefit of the business.

I have worked within the organisation for over 12 years and possess a breadth of experience in team and project management. I am capable of improving internal processes to create more profitable and efficient working environments. With proven success in purchasing of raw materials and packaging for the Shipley site, I am an experienced negotiator and troubleshooter. I am capable of maintaining a positive and supportive attitude with diplomacy and good humour in order to achieve desired results.

Recent achievements within the business include:

- managed change following the introduction of robotic line equipment, minimising disruption to production and maintaining high levels of staff motivation;
- liaised with contractors, engineers and suppliers during the building of a £1m extension;
- negotiated best prices for raw materials with suppliers;
- Rationalised the usage of packaging materials, standardising the sizes of cardboard boxes across all three manufacturing sites, resulting in savings of around 10%;
- standardised the size of blue cheese manufactured across the three sites, resulting in a 10% reduction of waste;
- sold surplus milk securing profits of £120K during 2001.

I am committed to achieving business targets and the continuous development of the organisation. My experience and achievements would, I feel, allow me to create a positive impact within the role of **Purchasing Planning Manager**, and I would welcome the opportunity to progress this opportunity further.

Should you require any further information please do not hesitate to contact me.

Yours sincerely

Aidan Redbourn

Enc. CV

Analysing the letter

Aidan begins his letter by making it very clear what role he is applying for and very importantly, he has addressed the letter to the appropriate person.

He then expresses his breadth of experience with the XYZ Dairy; it is essential to highlight this point early on as it is likely that this position will be open to external candidates. Internal candidates are often favoured above external candidates for two reasons: one, an organisation that progresses one's employees is more likely to maintain a motivated workforce; two, hiring someone internally is the cheaper option, saving the company expensive finder's fees.

The job specification specifies that the ideal candidate will have experience in a purchasing/planning role in the food manufacturing industry. Accordingly, Aidan proceeds to highlight his purchasing experience within food manufacturing.

In the subsequent paragraph Aidan emphasises some of his recent achievements, providing his reader with demonstrable examples of his negotiation and communication skills, and his ability to devise and implement cost saving initiatives.

He concludes his letter by stressing his commitment to achieving business targets and developing XYZ Dairy.

Outcome

Aidan focused on articulating why he was a strong candidate for this position and ensured he matched his skills and experience closely to the job specification. A cover letter is a fantastic way of drawing the reader's attention to your suitability for a role. Not surprisingly, Aidan was invited for interview.

EXAMPLE 4 – SAM DUBE

Sam was seeking to secure a place on an MBA Executive Programme with a leading business school, despite having no first degree.

Specification

ABC UNIVERSITY

Master of Business Administration (Executive)

Entry Requirements:

In order to apply, you will need to have a good first degree or a recognised professional qualification and at least three years' postgraduate work experience at a managerial level. If you have not completed a first degree but are able to demonstrate several years' managerial experience at a senior level, your application will be considered.

Should English not be your first language, you will need to demonstrate a high level of competence in English Language.

Breaking down what the university is looking for
The applicant **must have**:

- a good first degree or a recognised professional qualification. Alternatively, needs to demonstrate several years' managerial experience at a senior level;
- at least three years' postgraduate work experience at a managerial level;
- a high level of competence with the English Language.

The next page provides the actual copy of the letter that Sam sent to the University.

Mr Sam Dube
21 Cherry Crescent
London
EC1

Tel: 07123 456 789

16/12/200X

Mr John Saunders
Head of MBA Admissions
ABC University
5 Westwood Road
London
SW1

Dear Mr Saunders

REF: Application for MBA Programme – Leadership and Governance

ABC University is recognised as one of the UK's most popular business schools and I would feel privileged to be accepted onto your MBA programme.

As you will note from my enclosed CV, I am an accomplished entrepreneur with significant work experience encompassing a performance record of starting up several businesses from scratch across a variety of industries and thereafter, managing them into viable, profitable concerns.

In 1997, I founded Granada Travel and Tours in Gabon, a travel/tour company involved in selling airline tickets, tour packages, car and coach rentals. More recently, I set up the same in the UK. The company is now one of the UK's leading travel/tour companies and a provider of money transfers to over 80 countries.

I am incredibly ambitious and feel that in order to achieve my aspirations more rapidly it is important that I receive a formal education. The reason I have chosen to study towards an MBA is because I believe it is a premier qualification that will provide me with a theoretical knowledge that I can then apply to my business, it will develop my management and leadership skills, and it will provide me with a good understanding of various strategic analysis techniques.

Having researched the various MBA programmes, I am assured that ABC University would provide me with a comprehensive theoretical introduction to the functional aspects of business. The key features of the course that particularly interest me are 'Strategic Marketing Management', 'Corporate and Business Finance', and 'The Economic and Global Context'.

I am confident that completing an MBA through ABC University will increase the likelihood of me realising my ambition to stand for president of my country and to venture into media.

If you have any questions or indeed wish to discuss my application further, please do not hesitate to contact me.

I look forward to hearing from you soon.

Yours sincerely

Sam Dube

Enc CV

Analysing the letter

Importantly Sam has personalised his letter and has made it clear what course he is applying for.

Sam begins his letter by expressing recognition of the University's impeccable reputation – flattery is always good.

In the second paragraph, Sam summarises his background and expertise, and goes onto to provide two examples to demonstrate this point in paragraph three. Using examples to demonstrate your skills or experience is very important.

In paragraph four he communicates why he is interested in this particular course and what the benefit of completing the course will be.

He then compliments the University further and expresses how completing this course will improve his chances of realising his ambition. This formula is the same when applying for a position, i.e., what appeals to you about the company and the role, and what the benefit of hiring you will be.

At no point does he draw attention to the fact that he does not have a first degree and although applicants without first degrees will be considered, the percentage is quite small. The point to note here is how important it is not to draw attention to anything negative or to any competencies/requirements that you do not possess.

Conclusion

This letter was well laid out, not too wordy and it covered all the University's requirements as outlined in their website. As a result, Sam's application was accessed by the University's academics and he received offers from two of the three universities he applied to, to attend the course.

SUMMARY

You are now armed with the tools required to create an interview-winning cover letter. Remember, a cover letter can be both the making and breaking of your application so be sure to allocate sufficient time to each one you write. Each letter should take you between one and two hours to complete. As with your CV, ensure you get someone to proofread the document.

There are many examples of both specific and speculative cover letters on the appended CD, as well as cover letter templates.

APPENDIX

ACTION WORDS

Accelerated	Contracted	Explored	Mediated	Restored
Accepted	Contributed	Extended	Mentored	Restructured
Accessed	Controlled	Extracted	Merged	Retrieved
Accomplished	Converted	Extrapolated	Minimised	Revamped
Achieved	Conveyed	Fabricated	Mobilised	Reversed
Acquainted	Convinced	Facilitated	Modelled	Reviewed
Acquired	Co-ordinated	Familiarised	Moderated	Revised
Acted	Correlated	Fashioned	Modernised	Revitalised
Activated	Corresponded	Finalised	Modified	Revolutionised
Adapted	Counselled	Financed	Monitored	Rewarded
Adopted	Created	Focused	Motivated	Saved
Added	Critiqued	Forecasted	Navigated	Scheduled
Addressed	Cultivated	Formalised	Negotiated	Schooled
Adjusted	Customised	Formed	Nurtured	Screened
Administered	Cut	Formulated	Observed	Searched
Advanced	Debated	Fostered	Obtained	Secured
Advised	Decreased	Founded	Offset	Segmented
Aided	Deduced	Framed	Opened	Selected
Allocated	Defined	Fulfilled	Operated	Served
Altered	Defused	Gained	Orchestrated	Serviced
Analysed	Delegated	Gathered	Ordered	Set
Anticipated	Delivered	Generated	Organised	Set Up

Applied	Demonstrated	Governed	Oriented	Shaped
Appointed	Designated	Guided	Originated	Simplified
Appraised	Designed	Handled	Overhauled	Sold
Approved	Detailed	Harmonised	Oversaw	Solidified
Arranged	Determined	Harnessed	Participated	Solved
Assembled	Developed	Headed	Performed	Specified
Assessed	Devised	Helped	Persuaded	Sponsored
Assigned	Devoted	Highlighted	Pinpointed	Stabilised
Assimilated	Diagnosed	Hired	Pioneered	Standardised
Assisted	Directed	Identified	Planned	Stimulated
Attained	Disciplined	Illustrated	Practiced	Streamlined
Attended	Disclosed	Imagined	Praised	Strengthened
Attracted	Discovered	Implemented	Prepared	Structured
Audited	Dispatched	Improved	Presented	Submitted
Augmented	Dispensed	Improvised	Preserved	Summarised
Authored	Disproved	Incorporated	Prevented	Supervised
Authorised	Dissuaded	Increased	Prioritised	Supplemented
Automated	Distinguished	Indoctrinated	Probed	Supported
Averted	Distributed	Inferred	Processed	Surveyed
Awarded	Diversified	Influenced	Procured	Synthesised
Balanced	Documented	Informed	Produced	Systemised
Booked	Doubled	Initiated	Programmed	Tabulated
Boosted	Drafted	Innovated	Projected	Tailored
Broadened	Drove	Inspected	Promoted	Targeted
Budgeted	Earned	Inspired	Proposed	Taught
Built	Edited	Installed	Protected	Tended
Calculated	Educated	Instigated	Provided	Tendered
Captured	Effected	Instilled	Publicised	Terminated

Catalogued	Elaborated	Instituted	Published	Tested
Categorised	Elected	Instructed	Purchased	Traced
Centralised	Elevated	Integrated	Quadrupled	Tracked
Chaired	Elicited	Interacted	Quantified	Traded
Challenged	Eliminated	Interested	Raised	Trained
Changed	Emphasised	Interpreted	Realised	Transferred
Charted	Enabled	Interviewed	Received	Translated
Clarified	Encouraged	Introduced	Recognised	Travelled
Classified	Endorsed	Invented	Recommended	Treated
Coached	Enforced	Investigated	Reconciled	Trimmed
Collaborated	Engineered	Issued	Recorded	Tripled
Collected	Enhanced	Joined	Recruited	Troubleshooted
Combined	Enlisted	Judged	Redesigned	Tutored
Communicated	Enriched	Justified	Reduced	Upgraded
Compiled	Ensured	Launched	Reengineered	Uncovered
Completed	Established	Lectured	Referred	Updated
Composed	Estimated	Led	Refined	Upgraded
Compounded	Evaluated	Leveraged	Regulated	Used
Computed	Examined	Liaised	Rehabilitated	Utilised
Conceived	Exceeded	Licensed	Remodelled	Validated
Conceptualised	Excelled	Linked	Reorganised	Verified
Condensed	Executed	Lobbied	Repaired	Viewed
Conducted	Exercised	Logged	Replaced	Visualised
Consolidated	Exhibited	Maintained	Reported	Volunteered
Constructed	Expanded	Managed	Represented	Widened
Consulted	Expedited	Marketed	Requested	Won
Contacted	Explained	Mastered	Researched	Worked
Contained	Exploited	Maximised	Resolved	Wrote

Index